Relational Ontologies

COUNTERPOINTS

Studies in Criticality

Shirley R. Steinberg
General Editor

Vol. 505

The Counterpoints series is part of the Peter Lang Education list.
Every volume is peer reviewed and meets
the highest quality standards for content and production.

PETER LANG
New York • Bern • Frankfurt • Berlin
Brussels • Vienna • Oxford • Warsaw

Barbara J. Thayer-Bacon

Relational Ontologies

PETER LANG
New York • Bern • Frankfurt • Berlin
Brussels • Vienna • Oxford • Warsaw

Library of Congress Cataloging-in-Publication Data

Names: Thayer-Bacon, Barbara J., author.
Title: Relational ontologies / Barbara J. Thayer-Bacon.
Description: New York: Peter Lang, 2017.
Series: Counterpoints: studies in criticality; vol. 505 | ISSN 1058-1634
Includes bibliographical references and index.
Identifiers: LCCN 2016041487 | ISBN 978-1-4331-3223-0 (hardcover: alk. paper)
ISBN 978-1-4331-3222-3 (paperback: alk. paper) | ISBN 978-1-4539-1723-7 (ebook pdf)
ISBN 978-1-4331-3928-4 (epub) | ISBN 978-1-4331-3929-1 (mobi)
Subjects: LCSH: Ontology. | Knowledge, Theory of.
Classification: LCC BD331 .T5125 2017 | DDC 111—dc23
LC record available at https://lccn.loc.gov/2016041487
DOI 10.3726/ 978-1-4539-1723-7

Bibliographic information published by **Die Deutsche Nationalbibliothek**.
Die Deutsche Nationalbibliothek lists this publication in the "Deutsche Nationalbibliografie"; detailed bibliographic data are available on the Internet at http://dnb.d-nb.de/.

29 Broadway, 18th floor, New York, NY 10006
www.peterlang.com

For my grandchildren,
whom I seek to pass on the lessons I have learned,
to help them see the world
as connected and whole,
as a living, breathing world in relation.

CONTENTS

PREFACE

I teach a "Feminist Theories and Education" course for the University of Tennessee, Knoxville (UTK), which I developed originally with a feminist epistemological focus from my own research interests in feminist epistemologies. I use *Relational "(e)pistemologies"* as one of the texts in that course, along with *Women's Ways of Knowing*; *Knowledge, Difference, and Power*; and *Education Feminism*.[1] In *Relational "(e)pistemologies*," I develop a theory of knowing that is supported by the classic pragmatists and gender feminists, with other influences from radical feminists, indigenous scholars, and postmodernists.[2] By "relation" I mean to emphasize *connection to others*, including other people and ideas. The connection is transactional in that we affect each other, dynamically and functionally, and each is changed as a result.[3] As Martin Buber described this transactional quality, relations are mutual.[4]

In *Relational "(e)pistemologies*," I develop a theory of knowing that is supported by the classic pragmatists and gender feminists, with other influences from radical feminists, indigenous scholars, and postmodernists. I argue that none of us can know what is True or Real, in a universal sense, and so we must all be content to continue to talk about "knowledge" and "reality" with quotation marks around the terms. This is why I put ( ) around the "e" in epistemology and refer to traditional Epistemology with a capital "E"—due to its assumption of Absolute Truth. I offer an epistemological theory that insists that knowers/subjects are fallible, that our criteria are corrigible, and that our standards are socially constructed and thus continually in need of critique and reconstruction. I argue that an epistemology that rests on an assumption of fallibility entails pluralism, both in terms of there being no Final Answer at the end of inquiring and also in terms of the need to be open and inclusive of others in order to help us compensate for our own limitations. My relational epistemology is a pragmatic social feminist perspective calling for active engagement, aiming at democratic inclusion, joining theory with practice (praxis), striving for awareness of context and values, and tolerating vagueness and ambiguities. I argue that knowing is something people develop as they have experiences with each other and the world around them. People improve upon the ideas that have been socially constructed and passed down to them by others. They do this improving by further developing their understandings and enlarging their perspectives. With enlarged perspectives, people are able to create new meanings for their experiences.

In developing this epistemological theory and comparing it to other relational ways of knowing it was impossible not to have ontological discussions seep into the work, our understandings of "reality." I use a metaphor of an Ocean as representing our "pure experience" as William James (1909) describes this, and fishing nets to describe our ontologies and epistemologies that help us capture our experiences and give them meaning. Imagine the world, as we experience it, is like a vast ocean. We must design a fishing net to help us catch up our experience of this vast ocean and make sense of it. Whatever net we use, however fine the weaving, there is so much more in this vast ocean of experience than our nets can ever catch up. When we cast our nets, much will overflow the top of our net as well as spill through it and escape back into the vast ocean. What we use to make this net are our theories of knowledge (our epistemology) as well as our theories of being (our ontology). We cannot divorce ourselves from epistemological and ontological questions, for they form the very weaving of the net we use to capture our everyday commonsense concerns. While my focus was on the epistemological weavings of our net for *Relational "(e)pistemologies,"* (let's call them the warp threads that run lengthwise) I could not avoid the weft threads that run widthwise and help to make up our nets. My position is that it's impossible to develop an epistemological theory that does not include an ontological theory as well. My desire for this book is to turn the net and look at it from the perspective of the weft threads, and explore how an ontological focus will help us to further understand the nets we use to capture our experiences that are woven with threads of relationality.

In *Relational "(e)pistemologies,"* we learn that a relational epistemology is supported by a nondualistic ontology that emphasizes we are w/holistically connected with our greater universe, materially and spiritually (whole and holy). I argue this connection is at a personal and social level, but also much wider, for I describe our primal experience as being one with the whole of the universe. Such an expanded concept of relationality includes within it the natural world in which we live, our biosphere. Consistent with Buddhist, Native American, and ecofeminist views about nature, I do not assume any separation between human beings and nature. I describe human beings as one with nature. In *A Pluralistic Universe*, James (1909) argues that the world we experience is more than we can describe. He describes our theories as incomplete, open, and imperfect. Concepts function to try to shape, organize, and describe this open, flowing universe, while the universe continually escapes beyond our artificial boundaries. For James and myself, the universe is unfinished, a "primal stuff" or "pure experience."

Summary of Relevant Literature

I am in conversation with many eminent scholars whose work contributes significantly to mine. My work on a *relational ontology* is grounded in the classical American pragmatist theories of James, Peirce, Mead, and Dewey. Allen, Bar-on, Cajete, Deloria, Farella, Lugones, McNeley, and Pratt are some of the sources for my cultural perspective. Sources for my feminist perspective include Belenky et al., Bordo, Butler, Code, Collins, Flax, Gilligan, Greene, Grimshaw, hooks, King, Martin, Noddings, Ruddick, and Warren.

Outstanding Features of the Book

Relational Ontologies is a concise, easy to read, yet detailed treatment of one person's ontological theory in comparison to other relational approaches. This will make *Relational Ontologies* a book that graduate students will find accessible, and yet it also offers high-quality scholarship, and numerous sources for topics and issues that students will want to pursue on their own.

Professors will find *Relational Ontologies* a valuable text to add to their class list of books. Due to its detailed treatment of current feminist ontological issues, it is possible to use *Relational Ontologies* as a central text in a course on feminist theories, ontological theories, or indigenous theories, and then give students assignments to research other individual scholars cited within the text on their own.

Relational Ontologies is a book that is timely and forward thinking; it also addresses major theories from the past which have contributed to the author's ontological theory. The timely quality of this book will make it possible for students to not only be aware of the history of ontological theories, but also help them understand the current issues and concerns being debated. From a professorial standpoint, this is also an attractive feature as current relational ontological perspectives are usually in article or paper form, or within an edited volume. Rarely are they found discussed throughout one text, as they are presented here.

Relational Ontologies will be a valuable book for professors to use in graduate courses that consider ontologies as a topic. This includes people who teach graduate courses in philosophy of education, philosophy, indigenous studies, science education, and women's studies. This relational ontological theory has a wide reach and is applicable to most fields of study.

As a final outstanding feature of *Relational Ontologies*, since my goal is to offer my own relational ontological theory, I sincerely hope that what I write will be a significant contribution to the scholarly discussion on ontologies. If I am successful at this task, *Relational Ontologies* will be a text for graduate students and scholars in the fields of philosophy of education, and educators will want to read it for its scholarly value and the contributions it makes toward furthering our understanding of relational ontologies. I believe that what I have to offer contributes to ontological theory and has a major contribution to make to educational theory.

Approach

As a scholar, my theoretical background is in philosophy of education, and my interests include: pragmatism, feminist theory and pedagogy, and cultural studies in education.

The Intended Market

Relational Ontologies is targeted for graduate students in philosophy of education, philosophy, education, religion, sociology, ecology, cultural studies, and women's/gender studies which are enrolled in courses that consider ontology as a topic. It is also intended to make a significant contribution to scholarship in ontology, from a pragmatist, postmodern, and feminist perspective, so it should be of special interest to scholars of feminist theory, philosophy of education, education, and women's/gender studies. It may also be of interest to scholars in philosophy, religion, science education, and indigenous studies as well.

Relational Ontologies is recommended for use as one of several equally weighed assigned texts in a quarter or semester long course or as a main text with students doing research on scholars discussed in the text, or others not discussed, on their own. It could also be used as a main text in a shorter version of the intended course, such as a six-week summer school session.

Notes

1. Barbara J. Thayer-Bacon, *Relational "(e)pistemologies"* (New York: Peter Lang, 2003); Mary Belenky, Blythe Clinchy, Nancy Goldberger, and Jill Tarule, *Women's Ways of Knowing* (New York: Basic Books, 1986); Nancy Goldberger, Jill Tarule, Blythe Clinchy, and Mary Belenky (Eds.), *Knowledge, Difference, and Power* (New York: Basic Books, 1996); and Barbara J. Thayer-Bacon, Lynda Stone, and Katharine Sprecher (Eds.), *Education Feminism* (New York: SUNY Press, 2013).
2. Examples of scholars who have contributed to my thinking in important ways include: Linda Alcoff, and Elizabeth Potter, *Feminist Epistemologies* (New York and London: Routledge, 1993); Paula Gunn Allen, *The Sacred Hoop: Recovering the Feminine in American Indian Traditions* (Boston: Beacon Press, 1986); Seyla Benhabib, *Situating the Self* (New York: Routledge, 1992); Patricia Hill Collins, *Black Feminist Thought* (Boston: Unwin Hyman, 1990); Jane Flax, *Thinking Fragments* (Berkeley, LA, Oxford: University of California Press, 1990); Jean Grimshaw, *Philosophy and Feminist Thinking* (Minneapolis, MN: University of Minnesota Press, 1986); bell hooks, *Feminist Theory* (Boston: South End Press, 1984); Linda Nicholson (Ed.). *Feminism/Postmodernism* (New York and London: Routledge, 1990); Nel Noddings, *Caring* (Berkeley, CA: University of California Press, 1984); Richard Rorty, *Consequences of Pragmatism* (Minneapolis, MN: University of Minnesota Press, 1982); Greg Sarris, *Mabel McKay: Weaving the Dream* (Berkeley: University of California Press, 1994).
3. John Dewey, *On Experience, Nature, and Freedom* (Indianapolis, IN: Bobbs-Merrill Co., Inc., 1960).
4. Martin Buber, *I and Thou*, Ronald G. Smith (Trans.) (New York: Charles Scribner's Sons, 3rd edition, 1958, originally published in 1923).

ACKNOWLEDGMENTS

I have benefited from help in many forms during the process of writing this book. My first thank yous must go to my family, for their support that is always there with me, and they suffer through endless conversations about the topics and issues I ponder, especially my loving partner and best friend, Charles Bacon. My two adorable granddaughters, Elizabeth Jane (Lizzie) and Louisa Scott (Lulu), have been my inspiration during the writing of this book.

This project began with a sabbatical in Europe, sponsored by Prof. Gert Biesta, while he was working at the University of Luxembourg, in 2014. Thank yous must go to Biesta for giving me an invitation that allowed me to be on location as a visiting scholar for six weeks in Luxembourg, and then for three months in Edinburgh, Scotland. Much of my background reading occurred during the time while I was in Europe. I also shared my metaphor of a fishing net with a seminar and faculty at the University of Luxembourg and I thank them for their feedback and suggestions.

I must thank my own institution, the University of Tennessee, Knoxville (UTK), and in particular my program colleagues in Learning Environments and Educational Studies: Kathy Greenberg, for taking over as program coordinator, and Scott Ellison, for taking care of the Cultural Studies in Education masters degree program while I was gone. Thank you to my department head at that time, Steve McCallum, for his support that allowed me the free time to go on sabbatical for eight months total. It was a tremendous gift of time!

Thank yous must also go to the doctoral students at UTK who stayed in touch while I was gone and kept me connected to their work: Brittany Aronson, Ashlee Anderson, Sheryse DuBose, Melissa Harness, Miranda Paulk, and Sultana Shabazz in particular. They gave me the learning community I was missing while on sabbatical. During the writing of this book, once back home, I have had the benefit of two research assistants, Melissa Harness and Alexandra Ingram. Special thank yous go to Alexandra for checking all my citations and quotations. I thank her for her careful read of the entire text to help me catch any typos and clear up confusion.

There are many others who have given me feedback and suggestions along the way at conferences and in my classrooms whom I wish to thank, although I regret I cannot name them individually. I have shared various chapters of this text with colleagues who have served as reviewers for me and given me feedback, in particular Gert Biesta (Chapter 3) and Jim Garrison (Chapter 1). Chapters 1 and 2 have benefitted from feedback by guest editors for special issues of journals to which I submitted them. The introduction and first three chapters have benefitted from feedback by conference program reviewers to which I submitted them in smaller, conference paper forms.

Bernard Woma, Fortune, and the Woma family in Ghana are again thanked for hosting my family and me in Ghana and sharing their insight and feedback with me. We are still in touch today, and Bernard gave my Chapter 5 a read. In November 2015, I was invited to be an external reviewer for Akalewold E. Kebede's dissertation and to attend his defense in January 2016. It was perfect timing as I was just reading material to help me with the Chapter 5 on African philosophy, and I am so grateful for that invitation to travel to Ethiopia. Thank you to Department Chair Gebregziabher Debeb, for inviting me to Addis Ababa University, and to the faculty and students in the Department of Curriculum and Teacher Development Studies, as well as the supervisor of Dr. Debeb's dissertation, Dr. Amare Asgedom, for your insightful questions about my work. Thank you "fresh doctor" Akalewold Eshete Kebede for your feedback on Chapters 5 and 6 and for the reading material concerning African philosophy you sent to me (and continue to do so).

It is due to my long retired and much missed colleague, Clint Allison, and his recommendation that I sent the manuscript to my earlier book, *Relational "(e)pistemologies,"* to Joe Kincheloe (a former UTK grad and student of Clint's) and Shirley Steinberg, as editors of the Counterpoints Series at Peter

Lang. They enthusiastically received that original manuscript, recommended it to their acquisitions editor, Chris Myers, and he accepted the manuscript for Peter Lang. *Relational "(e)pistemologies"* was published in 2003. Since then Joe has passed away, too soon, and now Chris Myers has recently stepped down as Peter Lang's acquisitions editor, after over 25 years of work for them. Thank yous must go to Chris Myers and Shirley Steinberg for their encouragement to follow-up *Relational "(e)pistemologies"* with *Relational Ontologies*, and for their patience as I worked on two other book projects and waited for another sabbatical and the time to do the necessary deep thinking for this one. I hope the wait was worthy! It has been a great pleasure to work with them, as well as the publishing staff at Peter Lang.

INTRODUCTION: WHAT DOES ONTOLOGY HAVE TO DO WITH EDUCATION?

The world of "pure experience," as William James describes it, is like an infinite Ocean and the fishing nets we create are a metaphor for our ontologies and epistemologies that help us catch up our experiences and give them meaning.[1] When children walk into our classrooms, even as preschoolers, they come with an understanding of the universe based on the "net" their parents, extended family members, and caring community use to help them make sense of the world. The world children experience at birth is a booming, buzzing, aromatic world that they learn to sort out and make sense of with the help of their care providers. The metaphor of an infinite Ocean and using fishing nets to catch up what can sustain us in/on this Ocean is one I seek to further develop for this Introduction. I capitalize Ocean to honor and underscore the spiritual quality of what I seek to describe. I will turn to James and others for help in Chapter 1. Here I want to make the case for why a better understanding of ontology matters for us as educators.

The Metaphor

Imagine the world we experience is like a vast Ocean and we are afloat on this Ocean in a boat, like Pi in *The Life of Pi*,[2] able to dive back into the water and vulnerable to having the Ocean's waves wash over us whenever a storm develops, always knowing we will eventually sink back into the water and become one with it again. Our boat isn't necessarily small like Pi's lifeboat, with only Richard Parker, a Bengal tiger, on board in the end; it can be many sizes and hold multitudes; maybe we are on boats the size of cruise ships or floating islands. We must design nets to help us catch up our experience of this vast Ocean and make sense of it. What we use to make these nets are our theories of knowing (our epistemology) as well as our theories of being (our ontology). There are multiple kinds of epistemological and ontological nets we can design, maybe even an infinite variety, some more effective than others, in terms of the amount of Ocean life they are able to catch up, some are more beautiful, some more durable, or more particular to their sought after catch. Whatever epistemological and ontological net we use, however fine the weaving, there is so much more in this vast Ocean of experience than our nets can catch. When we cast our nets, much will overflow the top of our net as well as spill through it and escape back into the infinite Ocean. We cannot divorce ourselves from epistemological and ontological questions for they form the very weaving of the nets we use to catch up our everyday concerns and give them meaning.

Let's call the warp threads that run lengthwise in our fishing net, our epistemological theories, and the weft threads that run widthwise, our ontological theories. Whatever "fishing net" we inherit from our care providers is woven with these threads as they crisscross over and under each other, helping us catch from this infinite Ocean of pure experience what we need to sustain ourselves, until we become one with the universe again. As a young child, we are not able to compare and contrast our given net to others; we take our net as all there is and are not aware that there are other ways of making sense of our world and other experiences that can be caught up in alternative nets. We become aware of alternative kinds of nets when we begin to have trouble communicating and relating to others because they do not understand the world the same way we do. As young children, we probably do not notice all that is spilling over the top or through the holes of our net; we take what our care providers catch for us in their nets as all there is in this vast Ocean. We walk into school trusting that others experience the same world we do and make sense of the world the same way. We do not leave our epistemological and ontological fishing net behind when we come to school. Neither do our classmates, nor the adults who assume responsibility for our care during the school day; all bring their epistemological and ontological nets with them to school.

Our care providers likely know that schools may use different fishing nets; this is why they try to find a school for their children that continues to strengthen the net they, and others, have worked hard to weave and give to their children for their survival. If they have a choice they will find a school for their children that reflects their epistemology and ontology. If they cannot find a school that they are comfortable with, they may work to help create one, as I did when my children were young, or home school their children. If they do not have these kinds of options, for various reasons, they will likely work to help their children make sense of the differing meanings they will experience in the school they must attend. They will arm their children with tools to help them repair and reweave their inherited nets, until they are old enough to make their own decisions about what kind of net they want to use to sustain them.

Another word for "ontology" is "spirituality" in the sense that first being (Being, or what Heidegger referred to as Dasein[3]) is not tangible or material, and is primal to our survival. In *The Life of Pi*, Pi turns to multiple spiritual sources to help him stay alive in the Ocean with a Bengal tiger as his companion. *Spirituality* is a term that many associate with "religion," and religion is connected to particular religious expressions such as Judeo-Christian, Muslim, Hindu, or Buddhist traditions. These are various ways to weave one's weft threads in our fishing nets. I use the term *ontology* and *spirituality* as synonyms to emphasize how significant these weft threads are; they are what help hold our worlds together and give meaning to our lives. However, I do not want to bring along with this description of weft threads a particular religious affiliation. I am sympathetic to common key ideas represented in major religions, such as those that help us live in harmony and peace with each other like the Golden Rule (Do unto others as you would have them do unto you.). However I am not sympathetic to other key ideas, such as hierarchical ideas of human beings having dominion over flora and fauna, or men having dominion over women and children. By not defining *ontology/spirituality* in terms of a particular religion, I am aware that there are some pure experiences spilling out of my net. I am letting them spill, in hopes that my definition helps to enlarge and make the overall net more inclusive. Pi begins his journey in the lifeboat by jumping overboard as soon as Richard Parker swims to the boat and climbs in. He is definitely not comfortable sharing the same small space with a tiger and makes a smaller raft for himself out of lifejackets. He suffers much in this watery condition before he is willing to risk trying to coexist with Richard Parker on the boat. I am not comfortable, yet, with all that comes with those long-established religions, I am afraid of what will jump out or be consumed, and want to weave a net that allows room for many who have been pushed out of strong religious nets. We will have to see how things go, what responses will be. Like Pi, I am leery.

Educational Connections

In the United States of America (USA), we say that we seek to separate church from state to keep the teaching of particular religious views out of our public education system. We seek to offer our children a public education that is not taught from a particular religious perspective. We may succeed in this ideal at some point in time, if we can untangle religious beliefs from ontologies; however, we certainly did not start the USA's public schools without a religious perspective. The founders of public education in the USA started from Protestant Christian perspectives with such laws as Massachusetts' 1647 *Old Deleuder Satan Law*, which explains why at the same time that public education developed in the USA, Catholic and Jewish private schools developed as alternative possibilities for parents not comfortable with the Protestant values being taught in public schools.[4] Today, we find more Muslim schools developing to represent Islamic views, and Christian schools increasing in number due to parents thinking that the public schools have become too "watered down" and nonrepresentative of fundamental Christian values. What I want to suggest is that even when we remove particular religious expressions and rituals such as prayer in the classroom, or the singing of religious songs at Christmas time, we cannot develop schools of any kind without particular ontological weft threads.

Let me give some examples to help us see the weft threads of ontology that exist in USA public schools today that were influenced by Protestant beliefs. I mean these only as simple examples; the complexity of various Protestant beliefs is beyond the focus or possibilities of this book. Historically, Americans started our public schools with the Bible used as a common text in classrooms, and children were asked to memorize Bible verses as part of the basic curriculum. A key spiritual thread in Protestant Christianity is the belief in "original sin," which was translated by such influential religious leaders such as Martin Luther and John Calvin to mean that children should be kept busy and supervised all day, every day, for "idle hands are the devil's workshop."[5] Today, many Americans still believe that if we leave our children with too much free time, they will be led astray and will "get into trouble." Consequently, our schools are designed with set times for starting and stopping, limited times for passing in the halls between classes or for lunch, with bells going off and buzzers ringing to let us know it is time to start, finish, etc. The days are long and frequently we hear calls that we need to make them longer as well as to add more days to the school year. We find recurrent efforts to take away children's unstructured time for playing, eating, and socializing. We persistently worry that we are not giving them enough work to do in school and continue to add to their workload.

This spiritual/ontological thread based on "original sin" is not one that is woven into other schools in other parts of the world, even with the significant spread of Christian beliefs. Other parts of the world have developed ontological threads that describe childhood as a time of innocence and emphasize that children need time to play and rest.[6] In China, students and their teachers have a two and a half hour break in the middle of the day for lunch, recess, even a nap, before coming back to school for another period or two in the day (K–12). In Japan, classical music comes on to let children know schedule changes, and the children escort themselves out to recess and back while the teachers go to their lounge for tea and a chat with their colleagues. The children are not placed in lines, alphabetized, and escorted by a teacher or teacher's aide down the hall with their hands behind their backs, as I have observed in the USA. In many schools around the world children are left in classrooms for recess or study time, for example, with no adult supervision. Not in the USA; leaving children unattended can get a teacher fired! We still believe: "Idle hands are the devils workshop." Unsupervised children will be led astray and likely "get into trouble."[7]

I do not mean to suggest that children in China or Japan do not work hard, or that there are not problems with their perfectionist values, or that there is not more complexity to their nets, but that their cultures have woven different ontological weft threads into their fishing nets to catch up what it means to "work hard." Confucian ideas about seeking perfection have strong influences in Asian cultures with an emphasis on teaching children the value of working hard and making continual efforts for improvement, once they reach an "age of reason" (usually assumed to be around six years old). The children learn the value of hard work, but not usually Christian views that children cannot be trusted to their own devises and must be kept occupied so they will not be led astray.

In this book, not only do I want to help us notice ontological threads we use to make sense of our lives, and how these shape our schools, but I also want to suggest other values that could lead to a possible reweaving of the USA's fishing net, which will also effect what we catch up in our nets, thus causing a reforming of our schools. In this Introduction, I will only sketch, but in the book I will reweave our net on a larger scale. Current efforts to improve America's fishing net, by tightening up our curriculum in terms of what we teach and insisting that teachers increase the time they spend on literacy and numeracy, for example, at the expense of other "core" subjects such as history, geography, and science, and the elimination of other "noncore" subjects such as music, fine arts, and physical education, are being justified on the grounds that these will help catch students who have been falling through our educational nets. Again particular values are being strengthened, at the expense of others. Again we swing "back to basics," and lose more children in our schools that were already struggling to thrive with what we harvest in the fishing net we have created. Current educational policy efforts are succeeding in making our current public education net even stronger and less flexible, less able to adapt and adjust to diverse students' needs and benefit from their diverse perspectives. It feels like we are letting *more* students spill through the holes of our nets and over the top.

Not surprising, many of the students getting lost in the USA's public education are being raised in families who do not embrace American (Protestant Christian, individualistic, capitalist) majority values, for example, such as our Indigenous students, and our Latino/a students. In general, students whose families embrace more collective cultural values struggle in America's individually shaped net. Indigenous students whose families embrace views that their kin include animals, plants, and the land and that these living beings are important sources of knowledge, struggle in the USA's net that positions nature as something to be dominated, contained, and made to serve "man." We hear cries of harm and warnings of the pain that these new educational policy efforts are causing to the very children policy makers say they want to help. The cries and warnings come from scholars who better understand more collective, collaborative, holistic ontological weft threads, many of whom were raised with those spiritual threads themselves and thus are able to better notice the differences and recognize what is spilling out and over the top of the USA's individualistic, separated educational net.[8] Again, the care providers for the "children left behind" must find ways to help their children mend their fishing nets, and repair the damage our latest policies are doing to the communities', families', and students' well-being.

I think our latest wave of educational policy initiatives are harming all our children, not just those "left behind," and are making the experiences of teaching and learning in USA public schools more miserable for those who manage to survive on what is caught in the net. I do not have hope for significant change unless people deeply reflect on their spiritual values, enlarge their perspectives by considering with generosity and care alternative weft threads, and develop stronger critical awareness of what is spilling out over the tops and through the holes of their fishing nets.

To help us enlarge our thinking and become more aware of what we are losing from our nets, I seek in this book to describe weft threads of nondualistic relational ontologies that emphasize we are w/holistically connected with our greater universe, materially and spiritually. This connection is at a personal and social level, and is transactional in that we affect each other, dynamically and functionally, and each is changed as a result.[9] As Martin Buber describes this transactional quality, relations are mutual.[10] However, this transactional connection is also much wider than between people, for, in agreement with Buddhist views, I describe our primal experience as being one with the whole of the universe.[11] Such an expanded concept of relationality includes within it the natural world in which we live, our biosphere. Consistent with Indigenous and ecofeminist views about nature, I do not assume any separation between human beings and nature;[12] I describe human beings as one with Nature. We come from our infinite Ocean and we will return there as well.

What would our public schools look like if they were shaped by nondualistic relational ontologies? Maybe public schools as an institution can never be shaped in such a way, but I'd like to try to imagine the possibilities. There are examples we can turn to for help. I am not the first to seek to imagine and develop a holistic educational space in which children could grow and thrive, and these alternatives can help us imagine more possibilities still. Let me sketch an example of models of education I hope to develop further within this book.

School Implications

Gregory Cajete offers us an example of a very different description of educational aims from what we currently find in the USA public school system.[13] Cajete wrote what may be the first book on teaching Native American children, titled *Look to the Mountain*, based on his 20-plus years as a science teacher at the Institute of American Indian Arts in Santa Fe, New Mexico. Cajete's people are Pueblos and he is from Santa Clara Pueblo, New Mexico. He is a Tewa educator, an author, and a professor at the University of New Mexico, and the director of their Native American Studies program. He is known for his efforts to teach culturally based science, with its emphasis on health and wellness, contrary to what he describes as a western approach to science that focuses on power, control, and efficiency. Cajete bemoans science that is taught without any spirituality or morality. He describes how we, with Euro-western roots, treat our Earth as "real estate" instead of seeing ourselves as stewards of the land. As a consequence, our Earth is dying, and we are in denial of what we have created. What he describes as "cosmology" is what I am calling "ontology." What he describes as science taught without any spirituality, I am describing as using a different kind of spirituality/ontology, as I am arguing it is impossible to teach science to our children without using some kind of epistemological and ontological net.

In *Look to the Mountain*, Cajete describes Indian education as relationally focused (Indian is his term). Indian education brings out affective, subjective, communal relations, artistic and mythical dimensions, ritual and ceremony, and sacred ecology. Sacred orientation to place is a key concept, with seven directions, the four cardinals of north, south, east, west, and above, center, and below. Indigenous orientation includes: "the Mythic (the tribe's language and culture), the Artistic/Visionary (winter element—deeply inward), the Environmental (connects a tribe to their place), and the Affective/Communal (summer element—outward, highly interactive, external dimension). Cajete sums up his description of Indian education as being about a journey "to find our face (to understand and appreciate the passions that move and energize our life), to find a foundation (work that allows us to find [reach] our potential and our greatest fulfillment), and to become a complete man or woman (to find our Life and appreciate the spirit that moves us)" (p. 68). According to Cajete, Indigenous education is taught through breath, language, song, prayer, and thought. "Much of the education is informal, taught through experiences, storytelling, ritual/ceremony, dreaming, tutoring, as well as through artistic expression."[14] The spirituality described in Indigenous education is not a religion, but rather it is a way of life.

In 2000, Cajete published *A People's Ecology: Explorations in Sustainable Living*, as an effort to further develop the concept of "sacred ecology." He focuses on over 30,000 years of Indigenous people forming and being formed by the land. He describes what he calls a "theology of place," with the same common set of principles as he described in *Look to the Mountain*. The foundation of Indigenous education is environmental, based on an understanding that the natural universe is imbued with life and sacredness. Peoples' effects on this land have to be carried out with humility, understanding, and respect for the sacredness of the place and living things of those environments. We find examples of Indigenous beliefs in their art (e.g., Pueblo cloud motif, Kokopelli—the seed carrier), in their lessons they teach children (e.g., origin stories that are guiding stories such as coyote stealing fire), told through dance and ceremonies, and lessons on how to live a life that maintains what he calls "the web of life" and teaches children the importance of sharing our resources (e.g., the "hunter of good heart"). Cajete teaches us about Pueblo journeys (over 10,000 years or more), and how their ontology seeks to honor relationship and reciprocity, not only for renewal and remembering, like Judeo-Christianity, but also to perpetuate the spiritual ecology of the world as a whole.

Schools designed to teach children their connections to Nature open their doors and windows to the great outdoors as well as bring Nature inside the classroom. They teach children about the seasons, and how plants and animals adapt to the changing weather and amount of sunlight. They teach children science through gardening, how to feed the soil nutrition through composting, how to grow plants so that they work together, such as the three sisters (corn, beans, squash), how to care for the plants and harvest them, giving thanks for what they have grown. They teach the children how to prepare and cook the plants as well. There are schools where children are growing organic edible gardens, and replanting native plants local to their particular geographic areas. There are schools teaching children about the water cycle and the need to replenish our streams, lakes, rivers, oceans, and signing the children up to help with waterway cleanup and water-conservation efforts. These are examples of the kind of science curriculum that Cajete recommends we teach our children.

What is happening to science in our public schools due to the educational policies passed in the USA (e.g., No Child Left Behind (NCLB) and Common Core)? At the elementary level, our children are spending one and a half hours on numeracy and the equivalent amount of time on literacy.[15] Science that used to be taught for maybe 30 minutes a couple times/week is now almost gone from the curriculum, along with geography, history, and other "electives" such as art, music, and physical education. 30 minutes of science or geography or history squeezed into a week's curriculum is not enough if one wants to tap into children's interests in their surroundings and to teach them to be stewards of their world. In our secondary schools students are learning scientific knowledge that can be tested at a national level, for example, genetics in biology; it isn't place-based knowledge. They are *not* learning about their local area and the flora and fauna native to their geographic place, for example, the kind of knowledge of their local area that draws them into science as a field of study and teaches them to love and care for their local environment.

Conclusion

What kind of fishing nets are we weaving for our children? What weft threads are we including and working to strengthen, and what threads are we removing or leaving out? It is so important to carefully re/examine these most basic ways of catching up what sustains us in our Ocean, as these weft threads affect our children's well-being and chances of survival. The weft threads we weave for our children will determine what they catch up in their nets, until they are old enough to re/weave their own nets. From an relational perspective, currently we are not teaching them in USA public schools how connected they are to this living, breathing, continually changing Ocean and how important it is for them to see themselves as stewards during their journey, prior to sinking back into the Ocean. We are continuing, even strengthening our teaching that the Ocean is something to try to control and contain, to measure and dissect, and take from for our use, not something to honor and respect, to see ourselves as humble stewards of, in a reciprocal, sacred relationship. Pi not only learned how to share a life boat with a Bengal tiger; Richard Parker and he helped each other to keep alive and survive an ordeal beyond each other's individual capacity.

Book's Plan

I have started with the metaphor of an infinite Ocean and the weaving of epistemological and ontological fishing nets to help sustain us while we strive to survive on this Ocean, before returning to that from which we came. I will be making the case for why a better understanding of ontology matters for us as educators throughout this text.

In Chapter 1, I turn to an exploration of William James's *radical empiricism* and his *pluralism* to consider his contributions to my Ocean metaphor. I compare his epistemological and ontological net to what feminist scholars are weaving, as I make the case that he is an important ally to relational ontologies.

There are other ways to describe the interconnected, relationality of our world that are just as powerful as the Ocean, and I use Chapter 2 to describe North American First Nations' ontological and epistemological nets in terms of the Land with the help of Vine Deloria, Jr., Gregory Cajete, and Winona LaDuke.

Chapter 3 will explore the metaphor of rhizomes, as described by Gilles Deleuze and Fèlix Guattari, as another example of a relational ontology. Deleuze and Guattari compare rhizomes to nomads and war machines, but they also show how we can find rhizomes in plants, in particular grasses and trees. I will turn to higher education in the USA, and European Union, to show how higher education as a social institution serves as a rich example of tree logic with studies programs such as cultural studies and women's studies serving as good examples of grasses. Overall, their rhizomatic model illustrates another example of relational ontologies.

If we look to the East we find the metaphor of Indra's Net, with the stars representing jewels in the sky's net, which I will explore in Chapter 4. Chapter 5 will consider describing our world's interconnectedness through the metaphor of webs, in particular spider webs, that come from African oral tradition. Chapter 6 will sum up the commonalities and differences of these various relational ontological nets and consider further what relational ontologies have to teach us about educating our children.

Indigenous nations all over this beautiful Earth have found various ways to weave their nets, and I pull from their wisdom to help us (Euro-westerners) better understand the dangers and limitations of our own epistemological and ontological nets. Reweaving our nets so that less harm is done to our environment as well as our loved ones will have to occur in all our social institutions: our homes, churches, work places, media, health care, food, transportation, and our governments, to name a few, but for those of us who work in schools, there is much we can do to contribute to the reweaving of our ontological and epistemological fishing nets.[16]

Notes

1. William James, *A Pluralistic Universe* (London and Lincoln: University of Nebraska Press, 1909, 1996); William James, *Essays in Radical Empiricism* (Cambridge, MA: Harvard University Press, 1912, 1976).
2. Yann Martel, *Life of Pi* (Canada: Knopf Canada, 2001).
3. Martin Heidegger, *Being and Time*. John MacQuarrie & Edward Robinson (Trans.), Foreword by Taylor Carman (New York: Harper Perennial Modern Thought, 2008; Harper & Row, Publishers, 1962, originally published in German, 1927).
4. Joel Spring, *Deculturalization and the Struggle for Equality*, 7th Edition (New York: McGraw Hill, 2012); Steven Tozer, Guy Senese, and Paul Violas, *School and Society*, 7th Edition (New York: McGraw Hill, 2012).
5. Frederick Eby (Ed.), *Early Protestant Educators: The Educational Writings of Martin Luther, John Calvin, and Other Leaders of Protestant Thought* (New York: McGraw-Hill, 1931; New York: AMS Press, 1971).
6. Catherine C. Lewis, *Educating Hearts and Minds: Reflections on Japanese Preschool and Elementary Education* (Cambridge, UK: Cambridge University Press, 1995); Harold W. Stevenson, and James W. Stigler, *The Learning Gap: Why Our Schools Are Failing and What We Can Learn From Japanese and Chinese Education* (New York: Summit Books, 1992).
7. Barbara J. Thayer-Bacon, *Beyond Liberal Democracy in Schools: The Power of Pluralism* (New York: Teachers College Press, 2008).
8. Michelle Fine, Reva Jaffe-Walter, Pedro Pedraza, Valerie Futch, and Brett Stoudt, "Swimming: On Oxygen, Resistance, and Possibility for Immigrant Youth Under Seige," *Anthropology & Education Quarterly*, 38, no. 1 (2007): 76–96; Vivian G. Morris, and Curtis L. Morris (2000). *Creating Caring and Nurturing Educational Environments for African American Children* (Westport, Conn: Bergin and Garvey, 2000); Gloria Valdès, *Con Respecto: Bridging the Distances Between Culturally Diverse Families and Schools* (New York: Teachers College Press, 1996); Angela Valenzuela. *Subtractive Schooling: U.S.—Mexican Youth and the Politics of Caring* (Albany, New York: SUNY Press, 1999).
9. John Dewey, *On Experience, Nature, and Freedom* (Indianapolis, IN: Bobbs-Merrill Co., Inc., 1960).
10. Martin Buber, *I and Thou*, Ronald G. Smith (Trans.) (New York: Charles Scribner's Sons, 3rd edition, 1923, 1958).
11. Ayya Khema, *Be an Island: The Buddhist Practice of Inner Peace* (Boston: Wisdom Publications, 1999); David Loy, *Nonduality: A Study in Comparative Philosophy* (New Haven and London: Yale University Press, 1988); Paul Williams, *Mahäyäna Buddism: The Doctrinal Foundations* (London and New York: Routledge, 1989).
12. Paula Gunn Allen, *The Sacred Hoop* (Boston: Beacon Press, 1986); Ynestra King, "The Ecology of Feminism and the Feminism of Ecology," in *Healing the Wounds*, James Plant (Ed.) (Santa Cruz, CA: New Society Publishers, 1989): 18–28; Carolyn Merchant, *The Death of Nature* (San Francisco: Harper and Row, 1980). Val Plumwood, "Nature, Self, and Gender: Feminism, Environmental Philosophy, and the Critique of Rationalism," *Hypatia*, 6, no. 1 (1991): 3–27; Karen J. Warren, "The Power and the Promise of Ecological Feminism," *Environmental Ethics*, 12, no. 1 (1990, Spring): 125–146.

13. Gregory Cajete, *Look to the Mountain* (Durango, CO: Kivakí Press, 1994); Gregory Cajete, *A People's Ecology* (Santa Fe, NM: Clear Light Publishers, 2000). I use Cajete's language in his description of "Indians" and page numbers are cited within the text.
14. Barbara J. Thayer-Bacon, *Relational "(e)pistemologies"* (New York: Peter Lang, 2003): 259–260.
15. Brittany Aronson, "Critical Social Justice Teacher Education: Beginning Teachers' Pedagogy and Practice," Unpublished dissertation (Knoxville, TN: University of Tennessee, 2014).
16. A version of this Introduction was delivered at the Southeastern Philosophy of Education Society Annual Conference in February, 2015, titled: "What Does Ontology Have to Do with Public Education?" Thank you to the audience for their feedback in that session.

· 1 ·

WATER: JAMES'S PURE EXPERIENCE

Introduction

In developing a relational epistemological theory and comparing it to other relational ways of knowing, it was impossible to not have ontological discussions cross over into the work, our understandings of "reality." As we learned in the Introduction, I use a metaphor of an Ocean as representing our "pure experience" as William James describes this, and fishing nets to describe our ontologies and epistemologies that help us catch up our experiences and give them meaning. I have been giving credit to James for first developing this metaphor, but now I think that I may have given him more credit than he is due for the reason that I have not been able to find a reference to oceans in my rereading of James. I have reread his essays on radical empiricism and a pluralistic universe in order to prepare for this project and I cannot find the metaphor to which I thought he introduced me.[1] I see references to streams, as in *streams of consciousness*, and occasional references to nets, as in *our concepts are like nets* that help us make sense of our world, but something always escapes from them. For example, "(Y)ou can no more dip up the substance of reality with them (concepts) than you can dip up water with a net, however finely meshed."[2] But, nowhere have I been able to find a reference to *an ocean of pure experience*, although I could be missing it.

I've retraced my steps in my theory development and can see Kaufman-Osborn's influence, in his discussion of Richard Rorty's use of language as a filter that helps us catch up our experiences, and if we don't have the language for experiences, those experiences fall through our filter and are lost as experiences. Kaufman-Osborn uses the metaphor of "talking fish" in his humorous essay to try to show that "Rorty effectively 'forgets' that language is always relationally implicated in palpable webs of immediate experience that must be 'had' before anything caught up within them can be 'known' as a determinate subject of discursive inquiry."[3] Maybe I am giving my pragmatist readings more credit than is due and not giving my feminist readings enough credit for influencing my thinking? I hope to use this essay as a chance to further uncover and develop the net to my own thinking on relationality.

In *A Pluralistic Universe*, William James argues that the world we experience is more than we can describe. He describes our theories as incomplete, open, and imperfect. Concepts function to try to shape, organize, and describe this open, flowing universe, while the universe continually escapes beyond our artificial boundaries. For James and myself, the universe is unfinished, a "primal stuff" or "pure experience." However, James starts with parts and moves to wholes, and I want to start from wholes and move to parts and back to wholes again. This is an issue between us, I need to further consider, for while he describes himself as a *radical empiricist*, emphasizing the parts, my descriptions are in terms of w/holism.[4]

My aim for this chapter is to use this opportunity to explore James's contributions to my metaphor, and how I am able to consider him an ally for feminist theory. I will explore his contributions through his *radical empiricism* and his *pluralism*. I will then bring feminist scholars into the conversation and offer some critique as well as alternative ways to weave our nets. Feminists must always use caution with James; we can never fully embrace him due to his sexist views of women as "angels in the house." These views are derived from the context of his life and the times in which he lived, of course, but he was not able to critique his sexism in ways that John Dewey was able to do, for example, another classic pragmatist living during much of the same time period.[5] As a philosopher of education, my first exposure to James was his *Talks to Teacher* lectures he gave to Cambridge teachers, predominantly (white) women, in 1892. He warned them not to worry their pretty heads about psychological theory, he would wisely advise them on what may be useful and helpful for them to be able to better control their students' behavior in their classrooms and help the students learn.[6] Unlike Siegfried, who was able to overlook James's sexism for many years in her philosophical studies of his pragmatism, I couldn't overlook his patronizing tone as a feminist scholar working in a teacher education program with future teachers who are still predominantly (white) women. It was Siegfried who encouraged me to give James another look, as like her I consider myself a pragmatist *and* a feminist, although for me this was more due to Peirce's, Dewey's, and Mead's influence than due to James's influence.[7] In that closer look of James I found an important ally. Let's take a look at key ideas he has to offer us in weaving nets of relationality.

James's Pluralistic Universe and Radical Empiricism

A Pluralistic Universe

I begin with James's *A Pluralistic Universe*, which is based on a series of lectures he gave on radical empiricism at Oxford University in November 1907, and was published in 1909, the year before he passed away. I will put the bulk of my attention on this text as *Essays in Radical Empiricism* was published posthumously in 1912, with some of the same essays/lectures included in both texts. We will find in the description of James's ontology (his weft threads) that it is impossible to avoid his epistemology (his warp threads), as they crisscross over and under each other continually.

James focuses on spiritual philosophies for the Oxford University lectures, which he subdivides as pantheism and theism. Theism conceives of God as from eternity complete and sufficient unto himself. First we have the Absolute, then the World, and then Man. After discussing the collateral consequences of the essential dualism of theistic views, James describes how the world has changed with scientific evolutionism (Darwin's influence). James explains that he's going to ignore old-fashioned dualistic theism and focus on pantheism's two subspecies: monism (philosophy of the absolute) and pluralism (radical empiricism). He is going to argue that the philosophy of the absolute (the *all*-form) agrees with the pluralistic philosophy, radical empiricism (the *each*-form), as both identify human substance with the divine substance. However, while monists describe the world as one great all-inclusive fact, an absolute mind, God in his creation, James holds to a finite God, a pluralistic and incompletely integrated universe, and an antiabsolutist hypothesis. James does believe in God, but he tells us that for him: "*reality MAY exist in distributive form, in the shape not of an all but of a set of eaches, just as it seems to.*"[8] James warns us, philosophers don't embrace his radical empiricism: "the pluralistic empiricism which I profess offers but a sorry appearance. It is a turbid, muddled, gothic sort of an affair, without a sweeping outline and with little pictorial nobility."[9] It is messy! For me, that makes his theory immediately attractive. I will come back to the idea that philosophy of the absolute (the *all*-form) agrees with the pluralistic philosophy (the *each*-form) later in this chapter.

In his second lecture, James talks about pluralists going from parts to wholes, and he makes the case for a both/and logic, although he doesn't call it such.[10] He points out problems with an either/or logic, yes/no, black/white and makes the case for the value of *some*. Absolutism stands for all or none. James says: "Because the *names* of finite things and their relations are disjoined, it doesn't follow that the realities named need a *deus ex machina* from on high to conjoin them. [...] (N)aming the disjunction doesn't bar us from also naming the conjunction in a later modifying statement, for the two are absolutely coordinate elements in the finite tissue of experience."[11] For James, "Radical empiricism and pluralism stand out for the legitimacy of the notion of *some*: each part of the world is in some ways connected, in some other ways not connected with its other parts, and the ways can be discriminated, for many of them are obvious, and their differences are obvious to view."[12] James informs us that his own belief is in a pluralistic and incompletely integrated universe, one that is only describable by the free use of the word "some." Once again, this is the antiabsolutist hypothesis, and I am even more intrigued.

After discussing Hegel's influence in Lecture III, whom he describes as strengthening idealistic pantheism through his vision of a world of reason, and Gustav Theordor Fechner in Lecture IV, an empiricist pantheist, whom James thinks, offers a superior vision as well that contrasts to rationalists, James turns to the topic of compounding consciousness in Lecture V, and introduces us to Henri Bergson, a French mathematician turned philosopher. James tells us reading Bergson has made him bold. For him, Bergson's essential contribution to philosophy is his criticism of intellectualism. As James describes intellectualism: "(a)n immediate experience, as yet unnamed or classed, is a mere *that* that we undergo [...]. When we name it and class it, [...] (give it a what), all these 'whats' are abstract names or concepts. [...] (T)his power of framing abstract concepts is one of the sublimest of our human prerogatives."[13] Intellectualism becomes vicious when we begin to think that what a thing really is, is known through its *definition*. We forget that "concepts are only man-made extracts from the temporal flux."[14] Use of concepts become abusive when we cling to them even when they make things unintelligible. Feminists know this problem well, how historically *man* was used as a concept that supposedly was inclusive of *woman*, and how hard women had to fight to make the case that they were excluded from that concept.[15] Radical feminists helped feminists understand that even using the concept *women* is problematic.[16]

In Lecture VI, James continues his discussion of Bergson's idea of vicious intellectualism, and he seeks to address criticisms of Bergson's work, such as that Bergson uses concepts of his own to discredit the theoretical claims of concepts generally. Feminists are very familiar with this kind of critique (performance contradiction), and I will turn to examples of their responses below. James reminds us that concepts have immense practical use, they give us stability and order and a way to communicate with each other. Concepts have a map-making function as well. But, they also give us a static universe. They are "only moments dipped out from the stream of time, snapshots taken, [...] at a life that in its original coming is continuous."[17] Concepts are retrospective and postmortem. Concepts give us knowledge, but not *insight*. "A concept means a *that-and-no-other*."[18]

> So it is with every concrete thing, however complicated. Our intellectual handling of it is a retrospective patchwork, a post-mortem dissection, and can follow any order we find most expedient. We can make the thing seem self-contradictory whenever we wish to. But place yourself at the point of view of the thing's interior *doing*, and all these back-looking and conflicting conceptions lie harmoniously in your hand.[19]

Bergson's originality is in understanding that "(w)hat really *exists* is not things made, but things in the making."[20] Bergson gives us no closed system. He only evokes and invites. If we wish to know reality, we cannot know it by trying to bring order to the chaos as Plato and Aristotle sought to do, we have to dive back into the flux. We will never be able to logically define our universe for is it continuously changing. "Real life laughs at logic's veto."[21] Bergson turns us away from concepts and toward perception, a path Merleau-Ponty also chooses to follow.[22] For me, this description of concepts points to what we catch up in our nets, our ideas are like the fish and seaweed. Being able to catch things in our nets and name them is important, it stops the flux long enough that we can eat and sustain ourselves. However, James (and Bergson) reminds us that if we just focus on what is in our nets, we lose sight of the moving, teeming Ocean that continues on around us.

Lecture VII, on the continuity of experience, goes back to a discussion of one-many, the *all*-form and *each*-forms and how James's theory is a both/and approach, not either/or logically (my language). He uses a row of dots example, and shades, to describe how units of experience overlap, an idea similar to today's discussions of how our borders are continually crossed and our boundaries are leaky. James describes philosophy as "the vision of things from above" and he again defines his radical empiricism: "Radical empiricism insists that conjunctions between them (sensations) are just as immediately given as disjunctions are, and that relations, whether disjunctive or conjunctive, are in their original sensible givenness just as fleeting and momentary [...] and just as 'particular' as terms are."[23]

James concludes, Lecture VIII, by again describing God as a finite being, and arguing that pluralistic empiricism is a better ally of religion than rationalism. He reiterates that monism is the *all*-form, whereas pluralism is the *each*-form of reality.

> No matter what the content of the universe may be, if you only allow that it is *many* everywhere and always, that *nothing* real escapes from having an environment; so far from defeating its rationality, as the absolutists so unanimously pretend, you leave it in possession of the maximum amount of rationality practically attainable by our minds. Your relations with it, intellectual, emotional, and active, remain fluent and congruous with your own nature's chief demands.[24]

In sum, pluralism:

> means only that the sundry parts of reality *may be externally related.* [...] Things are 'with' one another in many ways, but nothing includes everything, or dominates over everything. The word 'and' trails along after every sentence. Something always escapes. 'Ever not quite' has to be said of the best attempts made anywhere in the universe at attaining all-inclusiveness. The pluralistic world is thus more like a federal republic than like an empire or a kingdom.[25]

James's humility and inclusiveness is welcoming indeed to diverse perspectives and interpretations, and thus he can be described as an ally who opens up significant space for diverse scholars of various persuasions and cultural studies scholars from various disciplines, to make their contributions and have their voices heard. James points out flaws in his fishing net and recognizes there is much spilling over the top and through the net he uses. I turn to his *Essays in Radical Empiricism* for further refinement of James's ontological and epistemologica net.

Essays in Radical Empiricism

In *Essays in Radical Empiricism*, a collection of James's essays on his ontology that was published posthumously, we find out in the editorial preface that the only summary of "radical empiricism" is in the Preface to *Meaning of Truth*.

> Radical empiricism consists: (1) first of a postulate, (2) next of a statement of fact, (3) and finally of a generalized conclusion."
>
> (1) "The postulate is that *the only things that shall be debatable among philosophers shall be things definable in terms drawn from experience. [...] This is 'the principle of pure experience' as 'a methodical postulate.'*"
>
> (2) "The statement of fact is that *the relations between things, conjunctive as well as disjunctive, are just as much matters of direct particular experience, neither more so nor less so, that the things themselves*". [Editor notes it is possible to be a pragmatist and not be a radical empiricist—due to 2 and 3].
>
> (3) "The generalized conclusion is that therefore *the parts of experience hold together from next to next by relations that are themselves parts of experience. The directly apprehended universe needs, in short, no extraneous trans-empirical connective support, but possesses in its own right a concatenated or continuous structure.*[26]

In the essay "Does 'Consciousness' Exist?" [reprinted from a journal essay, 1904], James describes "consciousness" as a function, not as a thing; consciousness is a function in experience which thoughts perform. "My thesis is that if we start with the supposition that there is only one primal stuff or material in the world, a stuff of which everything is composed, and if we call that stuff "pure experience," then knowing can easily be explained as a particular sort of relation toward one another into which portions of pure experience may enter" (loc. 149). This is where I interpret James to be presenting a w/holistic view of our world. He discusses neo-Kantians and the subject-object distinction. His contention is the reverse. "*Experience, I believe, has no such inner duplicity; and the separation of it into consciousness and content comes, not by way of subtraction, but by way of addition—the addition, to a given concrete piece of it, of other sets of experiences, in connection with which severally its use or function may be of two different kinds*" (loc. 170, emphasis in original).

Again we learn that concepts are mere *that's* which act in one context as objects and in another context as mental states. They help us organize our world, but they can take on a role that is greater than "organizing" if we forget they are human generated as a way of helping us make sense of the huge Ocean of pure experience (my language). This world comes to us first as chaos of experiences, just like the world of percepts. It's subject and object too, a simple *that.* There's no dualism in being represented and representing. His thesis is: "Consciousness connotes a kind of external relation, and does not denote a special stuff or way of being. *The peculiarity of our experiences, that they not only are, but are known, which their 'conscious' quality is invoked to explain, is better explained by their relations—these relations themselves being experiences—to one another*" (loc. 302, emphasis in original). This idea of relations being experiences to one another is important in a net of relationality, something I will return to below.

In "A World of Pure Experience" [reprinted from a journal essay, 1904, also in *The Meaning of Truth* (pp. 52–76)] James begins by reminding us "Life is confused and superabundant" (loc. 447). Taken as it appears, our universe is to a large extent chaotic. James compares his radical empiricism to transcendental idealism (Absolute Subject and unity of purpose) as presented by Berkeley and Royce and makes the case that for the transcendentalist his Absolute does not save him. Again we find James starting from the parts and moving to the whole as the second order. The metaphor he uses in this essay is a *mosaic*, but one that has no bedding. "(I)t is as if the pieces clung together by their edges, the transitions experienced between them forming their cement." James wants the metaphor "to symbolize the fact that Experience itself, taken at large, can grow by its edges" (loc. 833).

Ordinary empiricism has shown a tendency to do away with connections of things and to insist on the disjunctions (James explores this tendency through the work of Berkeley, Hume, and both Mills). Empiricism starts with particulars, the many, but cannot unify them into a whole. Radical empiricism is fair to both the unity and the disconnection. James gives *full justice to conjunctive relations*, without treating them as rationalists do, as being true in some supernal way. "Relations are different degrees of intimacy" (loc. 493, emphasis in original).

> To be radical, an empiricism must neither admit into its constructions any element that is not directly experienced, nor exclude from them any element that is directly experienced. For such a philosophy, *the relations that connect experiences must themselves be experienced relations, and any kind of relation experienced must be accounted as 'real' as anything else in the system.* (loc. 493, emphasis in original)

James says his philosophy of pure experience harmonizes best with a radical pluralism, with novelty and indeterminism, moralism and theism, and with the "humanism" lately sprung on us from Oxford and Chicago (Dewey). He's not sure if all these doctrines are necessary (loc. 853).

The essay, "The Thing and its Relations," was also published as Appendix A in *A Pluralistic Universe*, and as a journal article published originally in 1905. James uses this essay to defend himself against his strongest critic, Mr. Bradley, and considers this type of writing odious. There are three other essays in *Essays* that are responses to critics as well, and they also are odious and lose meaning over time. I have already shared from this essay James's definition of "pure experience" as "the immediate flux of life." Here we find that James also defines "pure experience" as "but another name for feeling or sensation." James offers a rich description of concepts in this essay as well: our concepts and our sensations are confluent, of conterminousness (things with but one thing between), or of contiguousness (nothing between), or of likeness, nearness, or simultaneousness (loc. 359).

I find James's description of his radical empiricism and pluralism frustratingly thin in these texts, which are mainly based on public lectures he gave, thus the format discourages depth of analysis. I find myself wishing for more, yet having to admit these texts are incredibly rich in what he does manage to catch up in his net and offer to feminists (in all our diversity): that the world we experience is more than we can see or describe; that nature is multifarious; that our descriptions of this world are incomplete and imperfect, thus requiring us to remain open to more possibilities and aware of the dangers; and that philosophy is guilty of *vicious intellectualism*.

Feminist Contributions

How could we *not* see James as an ally, maybe even a friend, with such important key ideas that he has to offer us? Seigfried is right to draw our attention to him, as have other pragmatists such as Richard Rorty. As I mentioned, we know the problems of concepts and how key terms like *human*, based on *man*'s perspective, leave *woman* out of the conversation entirely; she becomes invisible, or he speaks on her behalf, and her voice is silenced and/or coopted, distorted and misrepresented, misinterpreted or forgotten. Luce Irigaray does an excellent job of making a strong case that "woman" has always been defined in contrast to "man" as the inferior other, in her *Speculum of the Other Woman*. What should women do to avoid being objectified as subjects? "A detour into *strategy, tactics, and practice* is called for, at least as long as it takes to gain vision, self-knowledge, self-possession, even in one's decenteredness."[27] Because our concepts have come from man, as has our language, women must "speak only in riddles, allusions, hints, and parables" so that the language (man's language) does not clothe us in "cheap chivalric finery," and hem us in.[28] Irigaray's method is to combat and construct from the margins, for it is only from the margins that women can prevent any cooption and integration of their voices into patriarchal systems as they attempt to develop voices that allow them to imagine themselves in new ways.

Judith Butler is an excellent example of a scholar who has brought to feminists' attention that *women* was an important concept for feminist research, for prior to its use women were invisible, however *women* has come to be understood as a concept that represents a set of values or dispositions represented by heterosexual women, thus excluding lesbian women.[29] In her *Gender Trouble*, Butler warns us about the category *women*, like James warns us about concepts and how they can help us take note of different experiences, yet they can become normative in character and exclusionary in principle, and become vicious, dangerous, even tyrannical. Butler recommends that we dump *women* as a category and use the metaphor of *drag* to mock the expressive models of gender and the notion of true gender identity.

Other feminist scholars show us how *women* also became a category that represents white heterosexual women of means, thus excluding women of color and working class women, for example. Adrienne Rich combats the heterosexism of *women* with her concept of a *lesbian continuum* and Audre Lorde uses the concept of *the master's tools* to underscore the racism embedded in feminist theory; Donna Haraway uses the metaphor of *cyborgs* to deconstruct gender, and Gloria Anzaldúa draws our attention to First World colonization embedded in feminism with her concept of *la mestiza*.[30] These scholars all serve as excellent examples of contributors to feminist theory who have drawn our attention to ways that concepts can become vicious in their exclusion and fixation, and in need of critique and redescription.

We can find in feminist debates within philosophy of science and standpoint epistemology present-day examples of James's presentation that the philosophy of the absolute (the *all*-form) agrees with the pluralistic philosophy (the *each*-form). Feminists such as Haraway describe the philosophy of the absolute as "the God trick," or "the view from everywhere."[31] In contrast to a God's eye view of Truth, and I think in agreement with James's *each*-form, scholars such as Lorraine Code have argued for "the view from somewhere" or as Helen Longino describes this, "the view from many wheres."[32] Just as James points out scholars' embeddedness within their theories, Code makes the case that subjectivity is always there, hidden, despite disclaimers, and that we can always find the context that has been suppressed. Subjectivity is found in the examples selected for discussion, and the experiences used to represent "human thought," for example. Code doesn't want to abandon the possibility of objectivity, and she does not think that taking subjectivity into account entails doing so. Instead, she argues that subjectivity helps us guard against reductivism and rigidity. It allows us to accommodate change and let our knowledge claims to be provisional and approximate. Doesn't this sound like James's argument for the contextuality of concepts and, his critique of all/none logic for *some*? James also did not want to be viewed as a relativist, and elsewhere I have described both James and Code as offering examples of *qualified relativist* positions, similar to the epistemological position I take.[33]

Still, there is the worry that feminists' claims to some form of objectivity or agency in their epistemological theories are falling back on "master's tools", and we can see this worry come out in the debates about standpoint epistemology. Like James, Sandra Harding attempts to explain how it is possible to hold a position that seems an apparent contradiction in terms—socially situated knowledge. Her position is that all knowledge is socially situated (and James would agree), yet at the same time, Harding wants to argue "that some of these objective social locations are better than others as starting points for knowledge projects (to) challenge some of the most fundamental assumptions of the scientific (and philosophic) world view [...]".[34] Harding presents a reconceptualized objectivity as *strong objectivity* as a way to provide us with an account of how the world in fact really is, thus avoiding relativism. Strong objectivity requires that scientists (and philosophers) and their communities (the Subjects) be critiqued as well as "that p" (the objects of knowledge claims), but she argues this critique can be best done from the perspective of those whose lives have been marginalized by such mainstream communities. Harding parts company with James's radical empiricist view that experience *is* reality, when she moves from addressing the deep hostility philosophy and science have historically expressed toward women to claiming that those on the outside, those who have been excluded, have a better ability to critique scientists' (and philosophers) embeddedness. By expanding the community of inquirers to include outsiders, and thus maintaining a distinction between insiders/outsiders, she reinscribes the dualism James points to. She also is vulnerable to the criticism that she idealizes marginalized perspectives, by assuming they have more agency than dominant-culture perspectives. Bat-Ami Bar On and Uma Narayan are two examples of feminist scholars who have brought out these criticisms of standpoint epistemology.[35]

James thinks that the philosophy of the absolute (the *all*-form) agrees with the pluralistic philosophy he presents (the *each*-form), but I am doubtful that others in his time would describe them in such an agreeable manner. James thought that his radical empiricism was in agreement with his friend, Charles Sanders Peirce, at the time of their working together, but Peirce sought vigorously to separate his views from James's in fear that others would judge him to be a relativist, like they judged James to be.[36] Peirce clearly recognized historical contingency and context, the fallibility of inquirers, and the need to provide a method for achieving revisability of knowledge-claims, all in agreement with James. Yet, Peirce preserves a final grounding for knowledge claims in his postulation of real existents and external permanency that exists independent of human thought.

We can see that the *all*-form and the *each*-form might disagree with each other, and with James, through disagreements that have emerged today among feminist scholars in discussion of standpoint epistemology.[37] Helen Longino's present-day response to Harding is to suggest that instead of thinking of individuals as epistemic agents, she recommends that we think of communities as the primary epistemic agencies. If we "multiply the subjects" and treat science (and philosophy) as a practice, this commits us to viewing inquires as ongoing and theories as partial. Longino recommends that we recognize pluralism in the community as one of the conditions for the development of scientific (and philosophical) knowledge to help us eliminate individual biases, and she concludes that no segment of the community can claim epistemic privilege. But, Harding thinks Longino's efforts (and others such as Nelson and Potter) to make science better, more rigorous and careful, is not enough to eliminate the social values, interests, and agendas (the context) that are virtually shared by all of the scientific community.

We can make the case that what feminists need to do is get out of the business of trying to develop a feminist epistemology that uses the tools of traditional *all*-form philosophy (and science), such as epistemic privilege and objectivity, and seeks to claim Truth, and instead embrace the *each*-form James is pointing to. I have made this case already at much more depth than I am able to do so here.[38] My point here is that James's claim that the philosophy of the absolute (the *all*-form) agrees with the pluralistic philosophy (the *each*-form) is problematic, and not necessary to claim. James modeled his pluralistic views throughout his lifetime with a "live and let live" attitude for which he is famous, but it got him into trouble philosophically as he embraced contrary views as if they were on friendly terms when often they were not.

This brings me to the final point that I want to make in regards to James, the critique he tries to address for Bergson and himself as he embraces Bergson's critique of concepts. How can one use "concepts" to critique concepts without being vulnerable to the charge of performance contradiction? In fact, it is impossible to avoid this charge, as postmodern scholars have discovered, and James discovered long ago. Andrea Nye and Jim Garrison are two feminist and pragmatist scholars who helped me understand that it is impossible to avoid this charge, but the charge can be turned on its head by following James's lead and showing that philosophers can never get rid of their context in their search for Truth.[39] By reintroducing contextuality, one can show that it is impossible to argue for the self-justification of decontextualized foundationist epistemology without requiring a context to determine that it is not question-begging.

Nye traces the development of logic back to ancient Greece and demonstrates that while Plato appeals to transcendent Forms and philosophers' abilities to intuitively assess those Forms directly as his authority to establish True premises, Aristotle makes a different appeal. He needs a way to generate premises that are neither circular nor unfounded and finds a way out of this dilemma by proposing a new Being, the *cause*. The inquirer begins with the conclusion and reasons back to the cause: Given this result, what was necessarily involved in that effect? The answer to the inquirer's question is the cause. Aristotle's method is one of connecting logically from conclusions back to prior, more basic premises, which are intuitively more certain than the conclusions. Nye shows us that Aristotle's method is based on a trust of the inquirer's intuition to know what is more certain, until he arrives at what is most certain. How does the scientist or philosopher gain access, grasp, or intuit "what is"? Through his own direct perceptual experience. It is a method that allows us to reflect our own self-images—our perceptions—as Truth. "The great achievement of the demonstrative syllogism is not that it produces new ideas, but that it allows a man to draw out of his existing ideas, the 'cause' that shows why it is that what he thinks is true, must be true."[40] Aristotle wrote philosophical theory that mirrored the conditions of ancient Greek society because he assumed those conditions were natural and given, a society where women were not considered citizens, and their labor, as well as the labor of slaves, offered the Greek men, as citizens, the leisure of contemplation.

James's idea of "pure experience" is so important because it reminds us of all that our nets of epistemology and ontology do not capture, name, and give meaning to. It is true that the language we inherit from our social contexts has a tremendous impact on our lives. Language, woven into our nets, affects how we view the world and how we make sense of the experiences we have. It affects what we catch up in our nets. But, as Kaufman-Osborn reminds us, "the appropriation of meaning, no matter how oppressive, is always a matter of active transformation rather than mere assimilation."[41] It is also true that much of what we experience remains unnamed and cannot be reduced to its articulated meanings. Much spills out over the top of our nets, and through the holes in our nets. For feminists, the indeterminacy of "pure experience" is what makes "experience" so important to their work. Feminism encourages us to be receptive and attentive to the inarticulate too, not just what is named, which is why we cannot forego "experience." Language gives determinate form to what is nondiscursively had. Appealing to "experience" reminds us that no telling is ever the whole or final story. As Dewey explained about his use of James's conception of "experience," "(E)xperience warns us that all intellectual terms are the products of discrimination and classification, and that we must, as philosophers, go back to the primitive situations of life that antecede and generate those reflective interpretations, so that we relive former processes of interpretation in a wary manner."[42] "Pure experience" reminds us there is a huge Ocean, not just what is in our nets, "that the world which is lived, suffered, and enjoyed as well as logically thought of, has the last word in all human inquiries and surmises."[43] "Women's experience" helped us notice what was spilling out of the nets created by Euro-western philosophy and science, and it also has helped us realize all that is spilling out and not being captured by that concept.

A Relational Ontology

In *Relational "(e)pistemologies"* I describe James's radical empiricism as emphasizing a primal, integral, relational unity. I am not so sure that I am correct in that description now; my description may be more of a reflection of what I believe than him. It is clear that James describes our categories as additions to pure experience, not subtractions from. And, it is clear that James describes our universe as open and pluralistic, that there are multiple ways to describe it and that these continue to grow, as our open universe is one that is in-flux. James emphasizes the relations between things, and that these relations are experiences too. He tells us that the relationships can be conjunctive as well as disjunctive and that he emphasizes the conjunctive relationships between things as his perception is that philosophy tends to emphasize the disjunctions. James brings together what others tend to pull apart, while at the same time emphasizing *each* over *all*. I agree with James's description of an open universe, and that entails no Absolute final Answer. However, I find his pantheism/absolutism distinction problematic, in that he wants to go from each to all instead of all to each, for it seems to me that he remains *only* at the level of *each* as a result of this approach. He seems to get tangled up in his net and does not find his way back into a unified Ocean.

The weft threads in my fishing net describe us as going from all (the Ocean, pure experience) to each (afloat on this constantly moving Ocean, catching up in our human made nets that we cast out into the ocean what we can), back to all (as we notice all that is spilling out over the top and through our nets, that our nets are holey and in continual need of repair, that they are incomplete and can never catch up all that is there, and eventually that we will no longer be able to even cast our nets and will drop over the side of our boat and back into the Ocean). I embrace the possibility of multiple descriptions of this world, some better than others, but *all* of our descriptions are limiting and unable to catch up this world that flows on beyond our grasps. *We* are limited too.

I am not a theist or monist, I am a Unitarian Universalist who is more comfortable with nondualistic Buddhist descriptions ("big Mind," "beginner Mind," or *prajñä*) and First Nation descriptions (Spirit, Dreams, the Sacred Hoop, and Holy Wind) for what I think of as a unified *pure experience beyond differentiation*, than I am with "God." However, I recognize that what causes me discomfort and concern with God are the religious practices that have developed over time for Christianity, Judaism, or Islam, for example, which reflect the embedded social cultures of these practices. James's idea that relations are experiences to one another, and that parts of experiences hold together from next to next by relations that are themselves parts of experience is an important contribution to the net of relationality I am weaving. In this sense, perhaps I was not wrong to present James as offering a w/holistic description of our world, whole in terms of being unified, and holy, in terms of its spirituality.

Conclusion

It was my hope to use this chapter as a chance to retrace my steps in the continual development of my thinking on relationality, with a focus on ontology more so than epistemology. I also wanted to share with others the jewels William James has to offer and draw attention to his work for feminist scholars. It took Seigfried's efforts to draw my attention to his larger body of work, even though I knew James well in terms of his influence on American education. I have argued that James is an important ally for feminists who should not be overlooked. In preparing for this project I reread James's two key sources where he discusses his radical empiricism and pluralism, *Pluralistic Universe* and *Radical Empiricism*. To my surprise, I discovered that his description of the universe as unfinished "primal stuff" or "pure experience" did not rely on an ocean metaphor that I have been crediting to him. Instead, he places his emphasis on moving from wholes (alls) to parts (eaches) and gives little attention to moving from parts to wholes. I am not a radical empiricist as I start from wholes and move to parts and back to wholes again.

However, in redescribing James's ideas, I have come again to the conclusion that while we may be using different languages, referring to different examples, and placing different emphases on our descriptions, we are in fact describing the same unifying cosmos. I may refer to "pure experience" as being like an Ocean and he refers to streams and mosaics. Look closely and one can see each tile in the mosaic, or the individual fish caught in our net. Take a macro view and one sees a growing mosaic, or that there are multiple people fishing in various kinds of boats on this vast Ocean and they are using different types of nets, yet *all* of us are not able to catch all that is in the Ocean with our nets, and eventually *all* of us will dive back into the flux to become food for the fish we have been eating, one with the Ocean that is our universe, our cosmos, pure experience.[44]

Notes

1. William James, *A Pluralistic Universe* (London and Lincoln: University of Nebraska Press, 1909, 1996); William James, *Essays in Radical Empiricism* (Cambridge, MA: Harvard University Press, 1912, 1976).
2. James, *A Pluralistic Universe*, 253.
3. Timothy V. Kaufman-Osborn, "Teasing Feminist Sense from Experience," *Hypatia*, 8(2) (1993, Spring): 124–144. Kaufman-Osborn is responding to Richard Rorty, "Feminism and Pragmatism," *Michigan Quarterly Review*, 30(2) (1991): 231–258.
4. See *Relational "(e)pistemologies,"* Chapters 5 and 6. By "w/holism" I mean to emphasize whole and holy.
5. Charlene H. Siegfried, *Pragmatism and Feminism* (Chicago: University of Chicago Press, 1996). For Dewey, see, for example: *The School and Society [1900] and The Child and the Curriculum [1902]* (Chicago and London: The University of Chicago Press, 1990).

6. William James, *Talks to Teachers on Psychology; And to Students on Some of Life's Ideals* (New York: W. W. Norton & Company, 1958, originally delivered in 1892).
7. See: John Dewey, *Democracy and Education* (New York: The Free Press, MacMillan, 1966, originally published in 1916); John Dewey, *On Experience, Nature, and Freedom* (Indianapolis, IN: Bobbs-Merrill Co., Inc., 1960); George H. Mead, *Mind, Self, and Society*, C. W. Morris (Ed.) (Chicago: University of Chicago Press, 1934); Charles S. Peirce, *Values in a Universe of Chance: Selected Writings of Charles Sanders Peirce (1839–1914)*, P. P. Wiener (Ed.) (Garden City, NJ: Doubleday & Co., Inc., 1958).
8. James, *A Pluralistic Universe*, 129, emphasis in original.
9. *Ibid.*, 45.
10. I first came across that logical term in feminist scholarship, although I recently found it used in Deleuze's work. See: Lorraine Code, "Taking Subjectivity into Account," in Linda Alcoff and Elizabeth Potter (Eds.), *Feminist Epistemologies* (New York and London: Routledge, 1993): 15–48; Gilles Deleuze, *Difference and Repetition*, Paul Patton (Trans.) (New York: Columbia University Press, 1994, originally published 1968).
11. James, *A Pluralistic Universe*, 66.
12. *Ibid.*, 79, emphasis in original.
13. *Ibid.*, 217.
14. *Ibid.*, 218.
15. Sandra Harding, "Rethinking Standpoint Epistemology: What is 'Strong Objectivity'?" in Linda Alcoff and Elizabeth Potter (Eds.), *Feminist Epistemologies* (New York: Routledge, 1993): 49–82; Helen Longino, "Subjects, Power and Knowledge: Descriptions and Prescription in Feminist Philosophies of Science," in *Feminist Epistemologies*, 101–120; Lynn H. Nelson, "Epistemological Communities," in *Feminist Epistemologies*, 121–159; Elizabeth Potter, "Gender and Epistemic Negotiation," in *Feminist Epistemologies*, 161–186.
16. Judith Butler, *Gender Trouble* (New York: Routledge, 1990), Luce Irigaray, *Speculum of the Other Woman*, G. Gill (Trans.) (Ithaca, NY: Cornell University Press, 1985, originally published 1974).
17. James, *A Pluralistic Universe*, 235.
18. *Ibid.*, 253, emphasis in original.
19. *Ibid.*, 262, emphasis in original.
20. *Ibid.*, 263, emphasis in original.
21. *Ibid.*, 257.
22. Maurice Merleau-Ponty, *The Structure of Behavior*. Alden L. Fisher (Trans.) (Pittsburgh, PA: Duquesne University Press, 2011, originally published in 1942).
23. James, *A Pluralistic Universe*, 280.
24. *Ibid.*, 319, emphasis in original.
25. *Ibid.*, 321–322, emphasis in original.
26. James, *Essays in Radical Empiricism*, xii–xiii. William James, *The Meaning of Truth* (Cambridge, MA: Harvard University Press, 1975, originally published in 1909). My *Essays in Radical Empiricism* text is electronic, and citations will be made within my narrative as they are cited electronically by location, rather than by page numbers.
27. Irigaray, *Speculum*, 136, emphasis in original.
28. *Ibid.*, 143.

29. Butler, *Gender Trouble*.
30. Gloria Anzaldúa (Ed.), *Making Face, Making Soul = Haciendo Caras: Creative and Critical Perspectives by Feminists of Color* (San Francisco, CA: Aunt Lute Foundation Books, 1990); Donna Haraway, *Simians, Cyborgs, and Women: The Reinvention of Nature* (New York: Routledge, 1991); Audre Lorde, "The Master's Tools Will Never Dismantle the Master's House," in Cherríe Moraga & Gloria Anzaldúa (Eds.), *This Bridge Called My Back* (New York: Kitchen Table/Women of Color Press, 1990): 98–101; Adrienne Rich, "Compulsion, Heterosexuality, and Lesbian Experience," *Signs: Journal of Women in Culture and Society*, 5(3) (1980, Spring): 631–660.
31. Haraway, *Simians*.
32. Code, "Taking Subjectivity into Account;" Longino, "Subjects, Power and Knowledge."
33. Thayer-Bacon, *Relational "(e)pistemologies*."
34. Harding, "Rethinking Standpoint Epistemology," 69.
35. Bat-Ami Bar On, "Marginality and Epistemic Privilege," in Linda Alcoff and Elizabeth Potter (Eds.), *Feminist Epistemologies* (New York: Routledge, 1993): 83–100; Uma Narayan, "The Project of Feminist Epistemology," in Alison Jaggar and Susan R. Bordo (Eds.), *Gender/Body/Knowledge* (New Brunswick, NJ: Rutgers University Press, 1989): 256–272.
36. Peirce, *Values in a Universe of Chance*.
37. Longino, "Subjects, Power and Knowledge;" Harding, "Rethinking Standpoint Epistemology."
38. Thayer-Bacon, *Relational "(e)pistemologies*."
39. Jim Garrison, "Dangerous Dualisms in Siegel's Theory of Critical Thinking: A Deweyan Pragmatist Responds," *Journal of Philosophy of Education*, 33(2) (1999a): 213–232; Jim Garrison, "Reclaiming the Lógos, Considering the Consequences, and Restoring Context," *Educational Theory*, 49(3) (1999b): 317–337; Andrea Nye, *Words of Power: A Feminist Reading of the History of Logic* (New York: Routledge, 1990).
40. Nye, 58.
41. Kaufman-Osborn, 1993, p. 133. See Chapter 1 of Thayer-Bacon, *Relational "(e)pistemologies*" for more discussion of this point.
42. Dewey, *On Experience, Nature, and Freedom*, 386.
43. *Ibid*., 372.
44. A version of this chapter was published in a special issue of the journal *Studies in Philosophy and Education*, 2017, under the title "Exploring William James's Radical Empiricism and Relational Ontologies for Alternative Possibilities in Education."

· 2 ·

LAND: FIRST NATIONS' EXAMPLES

Introduction

As we were reminded in the Introduction, when children are born into a family and community, they do not come into this world with a sense of the world already developed. They do not arrive with a road map to help them find their ways. They are initiated into their family and community; they are taught a language, customs, rituals, daily practices, and given meaning by their kin to help them make sense of the world in which they are born. That world is flooded with sensations that children cannot sort out or distinguish without our help. It is as if they are immersed in a sea of infinity, an Ocean of pure experience at birth, and they do not have a sense of distinction from that Ocean yet, they do not "know" what it means to be "separate from."

Over thousands of years human beings have created multiple ways of making sense of their world; they have developed creation stories and scientific theories, for example. We have multiple words to describe these ideas, and we give higher or lower status to them, depending on if they are our stories or another communities' stories that we do not value or understand as much as our own. The narratives we develop, which give meaning to our experiences of "life," are called "ontologies" in the Euro-western philosophical world.[1]

In other worlds they have other names, and the Euro-western philosophical world may classify them as myths, or religions, for example, not recognizing them as philosophical theories.

I am a philosopher, born into a United States of America (USA) military family, initiated and educated in various settings in the States and in other countries where the USA had a military presence during the Cold War era. My family (clan) has been living on the continent of America since pre-USA revolution, but they originated in what we currently call "the United Kingdom," in Scotland and England. I come from the Rae clan (MacRae). I use the word "ontology" to describe the theories we develop to make sense of our world, in terms of its essence, first meanings, or what some would describe as its spirituality. I will use the word "epistemology" to symbolize the theories we develop and the criteria we use to help us decide what counts as knowledge, what some call truth. I mean to emphasize epistemology as knowing, a process, based on criteria that are corrigible (correctible), and lead us to truths (not naïve relativism, but qualified by as much "evidence" as we can muster, depending on what our community defines as evidence). I recognize that we live in a pluralistic world where there are multiple ways to describe this world.

What I want to explore in this chapter and further develop is a fishing net I call "relationality," made from relational epistemologies and relational ontologies, as its warp and weft threads. I turn to peoples whom some would call "Native Americans," "Indians," "tribal peoples," "indigenous peoples," "First Nations," or more specifically Sioux, Cheyenne, Hopis, Navajos (Dinè), Apache, Cherokee, Puma, Pueblos, Klamath and Modoc tribes, Karuk, Yurok, and Hupa tribes, to name a few of the over 500 tribes in the Americas.[2] I mean no disrespect in my use of terms, quite the opposite, and to protect me from causing harm as a Euro-westerner, I will turn to tribal peoples' own words to help me describe and discuss their ontologies (spiritual beliefs). I am aware that many of the tribal names used above are White mans' terms, and that tribes have their own names for themselves.

The sources I have to turn to are tribal leaders who have written in a language I can access as a non-Indian, which is not their tribal native language, it is White man's language, English. However, it is not *my* language either. I also inherited it and find it constricts and shapes my thoughts in ways I do not like or want; it imposes upon me what I catch in the net I am using, as I seek to become more aware of the net I have inherited and try to help weave a better net for me/us to use, one that I sense is superior at capturing what I experience and seek to describe. I cannot find as many examples within my own native community that describe relationality as well as I can find from other sources. The fact that I cannot find many good sources within the Euro-western net draws our attention to the possibilities of misunderstands and harm done to tribal peoples postcontact with Euro-western peoples. I turn to indigenous peoples from the Americas for help, not as a tourist but instead as a world traveler and I hope as an ally and friend,[3] someone who seeks to honor the significance of indigenous peoples' already, longtime-developed relational nets.

Euro-westerners can learn from indigenous scholars, if we are willing to listen, and try to understand them. They have been trying to teach us about their relational nets for a long time, but we have found it very difficult to even hear, let alone consider what they have to say. To take seriously indigenous peoples ways of being requires a paradigm shift many Euro-westerners are not willing or able to make. It means to risk transformation. More recently, as worries mount concerning the ecological conditions of our world, ecologically minded scholars have begun to listen. I turn to three key indigenous scholars who have been seeking to help the Euro-western world understand their indigenous fishing nets and have written as well as spoken at regional, national, even international forums. They speak out of concern for the Earth, and the possible irreparable damage human beings are causing to "it" (our home). I introduce them by seniority.

Vine Deloria, Jr. (1933–2005) was born a member of the Yankton Sioux (his grandfather was a leader of the Yanton band of the Dakota Nation), but his father transferred their membership to Standing Rock after he became an Episcopal archdeacon and missionary on the Standing Rock Indian Reservation. Deloria, Jr. was educated as a child at reservation schools, and graduated from an elite college preparatory school in Connecticut, Kent School, in 1951. He is in a unique position as a Native American for he was able to obtain the degrees and licenses that the Euro-western world recognizes as legitimate sources of knowledge, thus making him "worthy of listening to," although Deloria, Jr. describes himself as "badly crippled" from too much education. Deloria, Jr. obtained a college degree in general science at the Iowa State University (after serving as a marine in the US military), he also earned a theology degree from the Lutheran School of Theology, and he was awarded a law degree in 1970 from the University of Colorado. He eventually became a tenured professor of law and political science at the University of Arizona in 1978 and was chair of the USA's first American Indian Studies program, which he helped establish. He taught at the University of Colorado, Boulder, from 1990–2000, and after retirement went back to teach law at the University of Arizona. It's clear from just this introduction that Deloria, Jr. was seeking Euro-western answers in our key fishing nets, Science, Religion, and Law, but he did not find the answers he was seeking. They were spilling out over the tops and through the holes of the Euro-western nets.

Gregory Cajete's (1952) people are Pueblos and he is from Santa Clara Pueblo, New Mexico. He is a Tewa educator, an author, and now a professor at the University of New Mexico, in addition to being the director of their Native American Studies program. He earned a degree in biology and sociology from New Mexico Highlands University, with a minor in secondary education, and taught science to secondary students at the Institute of American Indian Arts in Santa Fe, New Mexico for 21 years. Cajete (1994) wrote what may be the first book on teaching Native American children, titled *Look to the Mountain*, and he is known for his efforts to teach culturally based science, with its emphasis on health and wellness. Again, we find Cajete is in a unique position to serve as a spokesperson for indigenous education for he has the necessary, recognized Euro-western degrees as well as many years of experience working with children/young adults as an educator.

Winona LaDuke's (1959) people are the Anishinaabe (Ojibwe) and she lives on the White Earth Reservation in northern Minnesota, although she did not move there until she was an adult (1982). LaDuke was born in Los Angeles, where her father, an Anishinaabe (Ojibwe), was a Hollywood actor, writer, and spiritual guide. She grew up in Ashland, Oregon, where her mother, of Russian Jewish descent, lived and worked as an art instructor. Her parents were both activists for peoples' rights. LaDuke is also in a unique position as a Native American spokesperson for she is the first one to run as a candidate for the national office of vice president of the USA. LaDuke ran for vice president twice (1996 and 2000), with Ralph Nader in the presidential role, as the official nominees for the Green Party. She is known as a Native American activist, an environmentalist, an economist, and writer. She has a degree from Harvard University in rural economic development and a master's degree in community economic development from Antioch University. She moved to White Earth Reservation after college, taking a job as principal of the high school on the reservation, where she had to learn her peoples' language and earn their trust in order to be accepted there. She is currently the executive director of both Honor the Earth and White Earth Land Recovery Project, which she founded at White Earth Reservation in 1989.

We will learn that a common theme for all three of these indigenous leaders is the importance of preserving the integrity of tribal communities and applying indigenous wisdom to contemporary problems. It is this theme that gives me permission to turn to them for help. They position tribal peoples' accumulated knowledge of this land as available to help safeguard the planet, or using my metaphor, they help us understand that tribal communities have woven a richly developed relational fishing net over an extended period of time that does not harm our Ocean, but instead shows us how to live a sustainable life and then give ourselves with grace back to the Ocean from which we come.

I begin with a description of tribal peoples spiritual beliefs, their relational ontology, as described mainly by Deloria, Jr., with confirmation from Cajete and LaDuke. I will then contrast their relational descriptions to the complex Euro-western ontological net, as represented from their Native American perspectives. We will be reminded of the painful, disastrous results of contact between the two very different worldviews (two different epistemological and ontological nets got tangled up, with native peoples' nets being seriously ripped apart as a result). We will then learn of the mending that is occurring and the hope that more Euro-western Americans are finally beginning to listen and better understand that the epistemological and ontological nets they have inherited and helped maintain need to be rewoven as relational nets. Their nets of Science, Judeo-Christianity, and Reason are depleting the Ocean of the very life forms needed for their/our own survival. They are learning that they are harming their own home, the Ocean.

Our world is infinite and it can heal itself, but it may take the Ocean ridding itself of us/people for it to heal. If we (Euro-westerners) are wise enough to seek to understand and learn from our indigenous neighbors and kin, there may still be time to make the necessary changes and do the repairs. For the sake of the three generations that have come before us, our current generation, and the next three generations to come, I have to try; we have to try. After all, we all are connected and related, and we are in this infinite Ocean together.

Native Peoples' Fishing Nets

As Vine Deloria, Jr.[4] points out in *For This Land*, which is a collection of essays he wrote on religion in America between 1965 and 1998, indigenous peoples' share many religious beliefs that are common beyond the boundaries of the Americas, although his focus is with the Americas, and that will be my focus as well for this chapters. One common weft thread in indigenous peoples' relational ontologies is that spirituality is living and requires practice. The practice is a daily part of one's life; it is not something we do just on holy days, such as Saturdays or Sundays. The practice can include the rigors of fasting, sacrifice, and prayer. Tribal religions insist on developing and maintaining a constant relationship with the spiritual forces that govern human lives. The Pueblos stand out as an example of this daily practice as they are fortunate enough to still live on land that was theirs precontact (the Hopi and the Taos); the Navajos as well still live on their precontact land and still practice their healing ceremonies.

Deloria, Jr. was involved in efforts to create a Native American Indian Church, and to encourage Indians to return to their old religions. He wrote about present efforts to revive traditional tribal religions in an essay titled "Is Religion Possible?" (1992). There he described anger Native Americans were feeling about the wholesale appropriations of their rituals, beliefs, and symbols by non-Indians.[5] During the 1960s–1970s, he witnessed non-Indians embrace the use of tribal practices such as sweat lodges, the pipe, peyotè, and sun dances that "are now akin to county fairs."[6] Particularly angering was the superior attitude of non-Indians as they adopted these sacred practices and perverted them, the arrogant body language that tells Indians that they are "indeed a conquered people and that there is nothing that Indians possess, *absolutely nothing*—pipes, dances, land, water, feathers, drums, and even prayers—that non-Indians cannot take whenever and wherever they wish."[7] For Indians, Deloria, Jr. tells us, these are private affairs, not shared; they are religious experiences that are sacred. Indians don't preach; they practice.

Tribal peoples spiritual beliefs hold in common an experience of the universe as "togetherness, synthesis, and relatedness."[8] They do not isolate things, and abstractions are considered "stupid and dangerous, destructive of spirit, and reductionist."[9] They experience everything as related, and everything is circular (there are scientific theories that are beginning to express similar ideas: Einstein's theory of relativity, Bohm's solid state and particle theory, systems theories such as Lovelock's Gaia theory, and Margonis's coevolutionary theory[10]). Both Deloria, Jr. and Cajete, as we will see further, point to ways science has now evolved to the place where it is becoming more in agreement with indigenous beliefs.

Native Americans' attitudes toward peoples, lands, and other life forms such as plants and animals are ones of kinship relations. A simple but profound recognition underlies all Indian attitudes toward the organic world. Their relationship with their kin is truly democratic, they do not place human beings above animals, plants, stars, or the land, in value or hierarchical status. They are relationships of equality and reciprocity, with an awareness of what other animals sacrifice so that humans may live, knowing that humans will die and their flesh will become soil for plants and plants will be eaten by the animals. Such is the life cycle.

The land is given special status, like a motherhood relationship, but all living beings are like kin to native peoples. With this sense of kinship relations come beliefs of responsibility. Tribal leaders view their job is to protect their peoples and their kin (including the land, animals, plants) for seven generations, looking back to three generations, ahead to three generations, plus this current generation. Tribal focus is not on individual rights, as we find in Euro-western classical liberal philosophical theories such as Locke's (1680–1690) and Rousseau's (1968/1762), which contributed to the USA and French revolutions.[11] Tribal focus is on responsibility and duty in a communal sense. Deloria, Jr. tells us that the most respected person in old days was the one who gave freely of physical wealth and showed concern for the unfortunate. Once we know that indigenous peoples in America focus on responsibility and duty, and equality and reciprocity, it is easy to understand that they emphasize hospitality in their spiritual beliefs, which explains why they welcomed and helped first contact people from Europe upon their arrival to the Americas. They were doing what their relational ontology required them to do as moral human beings practicing in their daily lives their spiritual beliefs.

According to Deloria, Jr., almost every tribal religion is based on the land being considered sacred. "Indian theology demands that the sacred places of the earth be discerned and communities of whole human beings be allowed to live on them."[12] Land is not valued as "a place of historical significance" or for its economic worth; land is where indigenous peoples were guided and taught how to live by their ancestors, and where they seek that continued guidance. Land is their source of knowledge and spiritual strength. Tribes have especially sacred places on the land where their spiritual leaders go for guidance, on behalf of the entire peoples. The Judeo-Christian world has temples and churches where rabbis and priests go to pray and receive guidance to share with their peoples. For Islam the Iman is not a "go-between," believers establish their own relationships with God, but they also have sacred places they go to pray, such as mosques. All of these religions have especially sacred places such as Jerusalem, Bethlehem, and Mecca where believers will travel great distances to pray and seek enlightenment. For Native Americans there are especially sacred places as well, such as the Black Hills (SD) and

Window Rock (AZ). The Sioux and Cheyenne shared Bear Butte in western South Dakota, and Pipestone Quarry, in southwest Minnesota was shared by a number of tribes as the quarry provided the stone for sacred pipes. Salt Lake was a sacred place for many southwest tribes.

Deloria, Jr. teaches us more about the sacredness of land in an essay he wrote in 1991, "Reflection and Revelation: Knowing Land, Places and Ourselves." He explains: "revelatory places are known only through the experience of prolonged occupation of land [...]. Tribal histories, for the most part, are land-centered."[13] For those who have revelatory experiences, which is not most or even many people but instead only one to two people per generation (for example, Black Elk), they describe these experiences as intense and fearful, full of feelings of dread and foreboding. They tell us that they did everything in their power to avoid the experience. What they felt was a sudden awareness that one is being watched and should not be there at that sacred place. During revelatory experiences the first characteristic is that old categories of space and time vanish.[14] For Native Americans, sacred places require specific forms of communication and interactions, particular ceremonies. "The ceremony is a form of exchange of gifts and responsibilities."[15] "(T)he basic premise—that the universe and each thing in it is alive and has personality—is an attitude of experience and not an intellectual presupposition or logical conclusion."[16]

Deloria, Jr. (1999) recommended in 1992 in an essay titled "Is Religion Possible?" that "(w)e need to gather around our traditional people even more than ever before."[17] We need to give Native Americans the freedom to conduct ceremonies on behalf of the Earth and her children—no one is watching the store.

> We must be confident that in showing respect for our traditions we act responsibly. In a real sense we cannot 'revive' a religion for that is going backward. What we can do is respect religious traditions and allow them to take us forward into the future. This is all the old ways ever promised they would do.[18]

Gregory Cajete (1999) begins *A People's Ecology*, which is a collection of 13 chapters written by different indigenous peoples, with his own reflections on indigenous ecology and the lessons he shared with us in *Look to the Mountain* (1994).[19] Cajete confirms what Deloria, Jr. has described: "Indian people have formed and been formed by the land."[20] Their orientation to place is sacred, and a key concept (what I describe as a key principle in their ontology, a central weft thread in the weaving of their net).Theirs is a theology of place that comes from living on the land for over 30,000 years.

In agreement with Deloria, Jr., Cajete affirms that tribal peoples' "thinking, acting, and working evolved because of and through their relationships to nature."[21] Their view of our natural universe, which I am calling our Ocean, is that it is imbued with life and sacredness. Any actions by the people, any effects on this land, are to be carried out with humility, understanding, and respect for the sacredness of the place and all living things on those places. Cajete reminds us that we can see examples of indigenous peoples' beliefs in their art (e.g., Pueblo cloud motif, Kokopelli—the seed carrier), hear examples in their music, and feel it in their dance. The arts are a means of ceremony and transformation. Learning how to express oneself through art is a process of spiritual training.

We can find illustrations of key principles in indigenous education, which at its foundational level is environmental. Children are taught that daily activities they participate in and/or enjoy the fruits of spiritual acts, such as hunting. They are taught the importance of being "hunters of good heart," and thanking animals for giving their lives to keep us alive, and that we will give our lives as well to them as part of the circle of life. Our relationships with plants are sacred too, for example, corn for Pueblo people. The Pueblos journeyed over 10,000 years or more, to their current location, and they continue to honor their relationship to corn, and the principle of reciprocity, "not only for renewal and remembering" as we find with Judeo-Christian religious expressions such as the Eucharist, "but also to perpetuate the spiritual ecology of the world as a whole."[22] Plants are not only for eating, but also for healing. Food is tied to culture and sacred rituals and ceremonies are tied to food. Practices of feasting, sharing, and exchanging foods reflect common ideas of sharing, reciprocity, community, and relationship to all life.

Cajete tells us in *Native Science*: "The manifestations and roots of the Native science of democracy run much deeper than the modern American political version of democracy today in that all of nature, not only humans, has rights."[23] Native American cosmology is inclusive. Rituals (e.g., festivals, dances, ceremonies, and the telling of creation stories) are all ways to remember the basic principles of the tribe—and pass these on to the children. In Euro-western philosophical language, these basic principles are key ontological concepts for the tribes, or what I am describing as important weft threads in their fishing net.

Cajete calls to us to educate our children and teach them to maintain what he refers to as the web of life. (In my language, it is a call to maintain our relational fishing nets.) He warns us "that the depth of our ancient human participation with nature has been lost and must be regained. The cosmological and philosophical must once again be 'rooted' in a life-centered, lived experience of the natural world."[24] We will return to him in section three and learn more about current efforts to recover indigenous knowledge and replant the ancient seeds.

In *Recovering the Sacred*, Winona LaDuke describes, in agreement with Deloria, Jr. and Cajete, that native peoples rituals are a way to reaffirm human relationships to the Creator.[25] They express their thankfulness to Creation and their understanding of the sacredness of the land in prayer, including songs. She also describes that mutuality and respect, give and take, are part of their tradition. Growing food is part of native peoples ceremonies and ways of life, like corn, and the three sisters (corn, beans, and squash), especially in the southwest area, and wild rice, in the Minnesota 6,000 lakes area. LaDuke shares with us current ways that tribal peoples are reclaiming wild rice in Minnesota, and retaining their fishing and water rights in Klamath land (southern Oregon), for example, and I will come back to these examples in the third section. She will be most helpful in teaching us about current conditions and where change is occurring. We will learn about hopeful signs that show that Native Americans are mending their nets and Euro-Americans are contributing to the mending.

It is my sincere hope that I have succeeded in describing key principles of indigenous peoples relational ontologies from within their perspectives, in their words. It is vital that their words and mine are received with as much respect and care as possible by Euro-westerners in particular, for what comes next is a very painful story of disrespect, dishonesty, violence, and incredible harm, even genocide. The actions of my Euro-western ancestors are not something for which I can ever apologize enough, even though it was my ancestors' actions, not my own. What I, and others with Euro-western heritage, can do is help with the healing and recovery work, and give back to our kin what we stole, in our betrayal of their trust and what they took to be our sacred word.

Euro-western Fishing Nets

When Euro-western explorers "discovered" the Americas and came in contact with the indigenous peoples already living there, many early contact explorers and colonizers were not able or willing to try to understand indigenous ways of living and their spiritual beliefs. Some were able to appreciate their wisdom and beauty, and the sustainable lives they were living, but most saw the peoples they met as "primitive," "childlike and naïve," or as "dangerous," even "savage." Because they did not have written languages, laws, religions, or customs they were viewed as "lawless" and "uncivilized" (yet governed so well that Benjamin Franklin encouraged the revolutionary colonist leaders to use the Iroquois League as a model for the USA constitution[26]). Deloria, Jr. tells us in *For This Land* that since contact, the tribal peoples of the Americas have struggled for the conferring of dignity for Native spirituality. Euro-westerners described their spiritual beliefs as "animalism," and still do to this day.

Since colonizing and the formation of governments such as the USA, the indigenous peoples of the Americas have bestowed "dignity upon a government and a system of life with the expectation that this government and this way of life will come to an understanding and will begin to act with maturity and dignity toward them. It is a great embarrassment that such expectations are unfulfilled."[27] Native leaders struggle to understand that the USA government is not their friend; tribal leaders still believe in the Bureau of Indian Affairs. Deloria, Jr. tells us: "Indians will continue to understand the conflict between Indians and the rest of society at its deepest level as a religious confrontation."[28] Using my language, indigenous peoples have woven their fishing nets with weft and warp threads of relationality, but Euro-westerners have struggled to even name, let alone give meaning in order to fully understand their weft and warp threads, their ontology and epistemology.

Deloria, Jr. does not mince words. In an essay he wrote, "On Liberation," he tells us that any serious talk about liberation means "talking about the destruction of the whole complex of Western theories of knowledge and the construction of a new and more comprehensive synthesis of human knowledge and experience."[29] He is pointing to the need for a relational fishing net that we can use to help us capture up "(a) new picture of reality, a reality conceived as a vision and not as a series of related or connected ideas [...]."[30]

Indigenous scientific views are integrated relationships of attitudes and behaviors, circles of relationship, where "(e)verything becomes an aspect of everything else."[31] A significant problem for tribal peoples, in contrast, is the Euro-western assumption of "objective knowledge" made by "educated" non-Indians, and their use of cause-and-effect, linear reasoning, with history viewed as chronological. Euro-western scientists embrace a doctrine in the belief of ultimate knowledge and isolation, through continual subdivision of any problem, until it leads to certainty, absolute Truth. The result of this kind of approach to knowledge is that the individual is treated as primary, and the physical universe is treated as a giant machine.

According to Deloria, Jr., Cajete, and LaDuke, Euro-western science and technology peoples value power, control, and efficiency. They seek objectivity and causality. Their focus is about profit, economic development, and standardization. Euro-western scientists treat animals as if they are dumb, and the land as if it is dead. Euro-westerners treat land as "real estate" instead of seeing ourselves as stewards of the land. We now have seed companies such as Monsanto who have patented plants/seeds and developed "terminator seeds" that will not re-germinate in an effort to control the sale of seeds, seeds for plants that have a long history of growing on the land, much longer than any seed company. From a Native American perspective, science is being taught to our children without any spirituality, or any morality, and our Earth is dying. We (Euro-westerners) are in denial of what we have created.

Euro-western scientists have a history of treating tribal peoples as if they are savages and primitives, whose bodies, bones, and blood should be collected as specimens and placed in jars and on display in museums. Cajete and LaDuke both agree with Deloria, Jr. in his specimen description, and both describe in their books what natives call "the vampire project" (the collecting of Native American blood and cells, without their permission, under the guise of helping them with research about diseases effecting them such as diabetes). LaDuke tells us an estimated one million Native American bodily remains were held in public and private institutions such as universities and museums by the late 1900s.[32] She shares with us the story of Ishi, the last Yahi, and how it has only been recently that the national Smithsonian museum in Washington, DC finally released his remains and allowed him to be buried with his ancestors, which was his dying request to the two University of California anthropologists who were studying him. She shares other stories of successful repatriated human remains, but also describes how if an ancestor's remains are old enough the law doesn't protect him or her—s/he becomes valuable to anthropological studies.

It is not just human remains that Euro-western scientists have been collecting since contact, they have also been collecting items made by Indians that were for their daily living, such as their clothing and moccasins, baby cradle boards and rattles, baskets for food gathering but also items such as baskets considered important to ceremonies, healing, and rituals. LaDuke tells stories about regalia that was stolen, kept in museums, contaminated there, then returned to the tribes at great expense to them, only to find that they are now too poisoned to use and too precious to pack away. The items are a public health problem. The "spoils of war" stories are heartbreaking stories such as the collecting of war spoils from the massacre of Wounded Knee, where unarmed children and women and old, sick, dying men were slaughtered, and then whatever items they had with them were taken and sold or placed in museums, including the discovery that a child's foot was cut off and remained within her moccasin, as war booty.

The USA government and the Scientific-Reason fishing net of Euro-western scientists are not the only sources of great harm and destruction to Native Americans' relational ontologies. The Judeo-Christian church has also caused great harm, in particular Christian missionaries, who have no better record than our politicians or scientists. Vine Deloria, Jr. is an important source for a Native American description of Christian churches, for his great-grandfather was a medicine man from the Standing Rock Reservation who bequeathed his spiritual powers to his first-born son, Vine Deloria, Jr.'s grandfather, Philip Joseph Deloria (his baptized name, his given name was Tipi Sapa). Philip Deloria decided, with his father's urging, to become an Episcopal priest in the hopes that it would help his people to adjust to changes on reservation life. He eventually was appointed a priest (1892) and supervised "all Episcopal mission work on the Standing Rock Reservation."[33] In James Treat's Introduction to *For This Land*, we learn that by the time Philip Deloria retired in 1925 "he had secured a national reputation as one of the most devoted and respected priests in the history of Episcopal missions to Indians."[34] Philip Deloria's son, Vine Deloria, Sr., also graduated from an Episcopal seminary and became the first Indian to serve as a denominational executive, as Assistant Secretary for Indian Missions, an experience he found to be the most frustrating in his career. His first child, Vine Deloria, Jr., also attended seminary, Lutheran seminary. The family has a long history with Christian churches and efforts to spread Christian spirituality, mixed with "fierce cultural pride" and an "acute sense of justice."[35] Deloria, Jr. speaks about Judeo-Christian faiths as an insider, with authority.

It may come as a surprise to Euro-westerners to know that tribal religions are very tolerant of other religious traditions, although this tolerance is consistent with their emphasis on hospitality in their spiritual beliefs. They recognize their own limitations in understanding the great mystery that is the world, and hope for revelations from other religions. They know that they don't know what others may know, and this realization leads to great ranges of flexibility in attitudes and behaviors. A native clergy existed early among the

Choctaws, Cherokees, and Creeks, for example, with the Five Civilized Tribes (Cherokee, Creek, Choctaw, Seminole, and Chickasaw) favoring the Baptists and Methodists (the two strongest Protestant denominations still today in the Southeast, where the Five Civilized Tribes originally lived). "(S)ocial customs were simply transformed from older Indian meanings to newer Christian forms of gathering."[36]

Deloria, Jr. explains that tribal peoples live life in the here and now. He tells us that tribal peoples are easily identifiable, their power is evident, for they have a Holy presence that attracts people; they have placid, confident faces, a gentle humility. They are not boisterous and loud. One will rarely hear any criticism of Christianity among tribal peoples as they look for the good in everything. My experience as a researcher on the Navajo Reservation agrees with this description.[37] Deloria, Jr. lets us know that tribal religions (their relational ontologies) allow for diversity of faiths in ways Christianity does not.

In "Christianity and Indigenous Religion. Friends or Enemies?" (1987), Deloria, Jr. describes Christianity as "an imperialistic religion," for Christians tend to see other traditions as foes rather than simply as different, as inferior rather than as having their own integrity. Because of this intolerance, he concludes: "Christianity is the chief evil ever to have been loosed on the planet."[38] He says that he never met a Christian missionary who wasn't convinced Indians dwell in darkness, that they are intolerant of their religion and culture, and that it should be repressed as soon as possible.

Deloria, Jr. describes Judeo-Christian faiths as commemorative and historical, based on rituals that honor the past, for example, the birth, life, and death of Jesus.[39] He describes how they are institutionalized (through the church) and are based on extreme intellectualism. For Deloria, Jr., his experience of seminary was "more a hopeful bolstering of ancient dogmas and doctrines than a true exploration of man's spiritual problems and yearnings."[40] He found seminary to be elitist, assuming those who attended have an inside track in comprehending divine mysteries, and having little to do with life. Judeo-Christian faiths use as their means of social control guilt, cosmic sin, and revelations from prophets and saints. God is presented as a divine bookkeeper that keeps track of our sins and determines in the end if we will be allowed into heaven or sent to hell. From a Native American perspective, Christianity has replaced living religions with magic.

Christians describe the nature of the universe as "a good creation that crashed into evil," with the serpent tricking Eve into eating the apple from the tree of knowledge (original sin). For tribal peoples, the universe is good and nature is not evil, it is an active force that demands our participation. The universe is living, and the drum is its heartbeat; "everything is connected to everything else and everything is alive and responsible to its relationships in every way."[41] From an indigenous perspective, Christianity has little to say concerning land and nature, it is an otherworldly religion that is alienated from nature; it fails to understand the Indians' relationship to the land.

Deloria, Jr. explains that Christians describe the individual as isolated, alone. In the Bible, a clear hierarchy is described that positions God on top, human beings under God, and animals under humans, there to serve people. Within the hierarchy, woman is positioned below man, and children below woman, all in service to man, who is in service to God. From a Native American perspective, Christians describe individual responsibility as toward God to the exclusion of responsibilities to others. This description deemphasizes the family and creates an immoral society. Tribal societies have woven a relational ontological net that describes individuals within a large network of relatives, including other species, and they share between species what they experience, including dreams, ceremonies, and rituals, always with purpose and to seek wholeness in their knowledge and experiences. Religion is viewed as a balancing and healing process. The social control mechanism used by them is social shame, with shameful conditions viewed as brought about by human misconduct. Their spiritual beliefs lack institutional authority. There is an open expectation that revelations can and will be received by anyone in the tribal society.

What happened when contact occurred between Americas' tribal societies and early missionaries is a complex, troubling story. Contact explorers and immigrants to America understood their experiences in the context of Judeo-Christian religions. Many immigrants left Europe and came to America seeking religious freedom of expression. Native American's were told that the country was large enough that red and white men could live in peace provided each respected the laws and customs of the other. In 1787, the US Congress declared the "utmost good faith" would be shown to the Indian tribes on the continent. However, what followed was Manifest Destiny, the Judeo-Christian idea that the world was intended for a certain group of people who followed the commandments of Genesis to populate and subdue. Law and theology have mainly been the instruments of oppression for American Indians. As Deloria, Jr. says in "An Open Letter to the Heads of the Christian Churches in America:"

> You have never chosen to know us. You have only come to us to confront and conquer us. [...] You lack credibility. Not so much in what you do. You lack credibility in what you say.[42]

Native Americans made efforts to expand their relational fishing net: share, include, adapt, and adopt. But the only option the US government has offered them is to leave behind their relational nets, causing destruction to selves and community and homes, leading to extinction. Early missionaries were less inclined to be involved in political affairs of tribes. However, the Catholic missionaries in NM, AZ, and CA saw the Indians as serfs. From 1830 to 1871, the churches played important roles in the development of government policy for Indian Affairs that helped subdue the Indians rather than impartially guaranteeing justice for the Indians. They failed to carry out their promises in treaty negotiations. As Deloria, Jr. describes this, since the 1880s Indians have been confined within the boundaries of white individualism. Whenever they try to recreate their sense of community, the government blocks their efforts.[43] The USA government tried to impose an agricultural system on nomadic tribes and prohibited ceremonies such as "keeping of the soul," and "potlash," which only increased Indians feeling of being exiled. This caused great destruction, disorientation, and chaos. The federal government could not fathom a program based on the assumption that tribal religious ideas were valid.

Native religious expression was outlawed. As late as 1921, it was the policy of the USA government to prohibit the performance of Indian religious ceremonies, then in 1923 the policy became one of limiting it. When there was a resurgence of tribalism in the late 1920s, this caused the missionaries to oppose the Indian Reorganization Act and the Native American Church. In the 1950s, when Congress was aggressively violating Indian treaties, the church gave silent, powerful support of the policies, by not helping the Indians counter the destructive acts of the government. The churches supported the dividing of tribal lands as a way to split the clans and make it easier to convert tribal members as individuals.

Still today, missionaries living on reservations consider themselves experts on Indian ways and express intolerance and impatience toward the peoples with whom they are living and supposedly serving. Native Americans are not allowed to serve as leaders in the churches and are excluded from the ministry. The church leaders are afraid to allow translations of their sacred texts into native tongues for fear the doctrine may become impure.

Deloria, Jr. explains that even though Native Americans know that "white man's religion and his government are hollow, without honor and without substance," they cannot ignore the Christian churches as "they represent a tangible expression of whatever sense of morality or integrity American society has left."[44] They know that "God's chosen people" are responsible for destroying forests and animals, that they have no sense of stewardship to the Earth. They know from experience that Christians have no sense of pledging the faith and validity of their religion, with a corresponding responsibility to uphold the treaties they help their government negotiate with Native Americans. Deloria, Jr. argues, both religion and civilization require, for their fundamental integrity, the premise that one can be taken at their word for what that word spiritually represents. For tribal peoples, and the relational ontology they have developed over thousands of years, this means we have responsibilities to the Earth and its creatures. "Unless mankind takes its responsibilities to the world, and unless Christians take their responsibilities to non-Christians, as serious and critical calls to action, we really have no future."[45]

Today

There is more recognition of the wisdom of indigenous nations today, as there is also more awareness of the destruction human beings are causing to their home, the Earth. There is more widespread acceptance that our Earth is experiencing significant climate change due to human interaction with the water, air, land, and living beings in all those spaces. I am doubtful we (Euro-westerners) can say that we are able to experience our Earth with the deep spirituality that indigenous nations have been practicing for so long, but we are becoming more appreciative of the fact that we do not have all the answers and we need help.

There are examples of a growing awareness that we need to apologize for our ancestors' arrogance and help to right their wrongs. There are increasing examples of efforts by Euro-westerners to help their neighbors mend their relational nets, or at least stop doing harm, and reweave our nets to be more like theirs. We are noticing that much is spilling over the tops and through the holes of our fishing nets, that our nets will never be able to contain all that is in the Ocean, and that what we are catching in our nets will not sustain us in the long run. We are taking so much fish out of the Ocean it is losing the ability to replenish itself. We are dumping so many poisons into our Ocean, it is losing the ability to replenish itself. We have damaged our ozone layer, protecting our Earth so much, that the Ocean cannot regulate its temperature easily, and warmer temperatures are killing off coral that helps to regulate the salt level of our Ocean, causing even more damage to all that continues to live in our Ocean.[46]

There is much recovery work to do, and still today nonindigenous peoples struggle to understand the harm we continue to do to indigenous peoples' relational ontologies. We, Euro-westerners, struggle to understand their weft threads as spiritual, religious expressions that give shape and meaning to their lives. Deloria, Jr. informs us that American Indians are the most closely regulated group in the USA, "wards" of the USA government and yet "domestic, dependent nations."[47] He describes various laws passed by the USA Congress and Supreme Court since the 1900s that have harmed American Indians in their religious expression (examples include *Quick Bear v. Leupp* (1908), *Rosebud Sioux Tribe v. Kneip* (1977), *Lyng v. Northwest Indian Cementery Assn* (1988), and *Oregon v. Smith*(1990).[48] The trend has been toward secularization, a new "civil religion." Religious behavior must be justified on secular grounds in order to be protected today.

In 1978, USA President Jimmy Carter signed the American Indian Religious Freedom Act, declaring Congress's policy was to protect and preserve the inherent right of Native Americans to believe, express, and practice their traditional religions.[49] However, the policy does not protect the locations where many Native American rituals take place. It does not recognize the sacred role of land in tribal religious expression. The USA courts and government have not understood that Indian tribes are communities in fundamental ways, wholly defined by family relations, not by residence or individual beliefs or talents. Everyone in the Native American community possesses ceremonial and ritual knowledge, although only a few may choose to perform these acts. The knowledge is passed along through generations; beliefs are an integral part of the experiences of the people, past, present, and future. For Native Americans, it is the principle of the respect for the sacred that is important.

Deloria, Jr. (1999) explains in "Sacred Lands and Religious Freedom,"[50] there are three kinds of sacred lands. One level of sacred is where events occurred, like the Lincoln Memorial and Gettysburg National Cemetery, for Americans. Wounded Knee, SD, is such a place for many tribal peoples. Another kind of sacred has a deeper, more profound meaning, like the crossing of the River Jordan for Judeo-Christians. For the Lakota, Buffalo Gap in the Black Hills of SD, and several mountains in NM and AZ for Hopi, Pueblo, and Navajo are sacred places that mark migration and boundaries. A third kind of sacred lands are Holy Places that are Holy in themselves, where human beings have always gone to fill themselves with spiritual powers, such as Moses and the burning bush, and for Native Americans, Bear Butte, Blue Lake, and the High Places of the *Lyng* case.

These are all well-known sacred locations. Forever, Holy Men have gone into the high places, lakes, and isolated sanctuaries to pray, receive guidance from the Spirits, and train younger people in the ceremonies. When Native Americans were forced into smaller spaces and on reservations, they were forced to adopt various subterfuges so that ceremonial life could continue. Many of the sacred places were on public lands so that traditional leaders were able to work out informal arrangements with federal agencies. This has changed over times as new generations of personnel began to restrict access. Deloria, Jr., Cajete, and LaDuke tell us, these ceremonies are for the Earth's protection, and all its life forms. They are for all of us, not any particular individual.

In 1988, the Supreme Court decided in the *Lyng v. Northwest Indian Cemetery Protective Association* case in favor of the federal government, which wanted to put in a logging road that would have opened up the high country to commercial logging, destroying the isolation of the ceremonial sites for three tribes (the Chimney Rock area of the Six Rivers National Forest). Ceremonies that have been performed for thousands of years were treated as personal fads. From an indigenous relational ontology, even though few people use the Chimney Rock area, the well-being of the entire tribe hinges on their Holy men's success. Allowing a logging road through sacred land denied the possibility of the continuing revelation of the sacred in their lives.[51]

What the *Lyng* case taught Native Americans is that the 1978 policy, the American Indian Religious Freedom Act, has "no teeth," as it provides no legal cause of action. We recognize the Holy land for Judeo-Christians but not Natives. It also reconfirmed for them, the dominant culture has an immense appetite for natural resources. Deloria, Jr. informs us that "(a)bout all the Act accomplished was to encourage federal and state agencies to adopt more restrictive formal rules to inhibit the practices of Indian religions."[52] Christian churches applied for and received a great deal of tribal land, which can only be used for religious purposes. However, as Deloria, Jr. points out, they have a declining religious following. The courts treat the issue concerning land as a property rights issue and an economics issue instead of a religious issue.

As a result of the American Indian Religious Freedom Act, now when Native Americans raise the question of reburying human remains they have to prove their burial practices are central to their religion. Is it possible, we imagine, that they do not care about their dead, or that they do not take death seriously? Deloria, Jr. asks, and LaDuke and Cajete echo this question; why are only Indians required to present evidence of their spiritual (translate to Euro-western language: religious) beliefs? Indian burials are within the scope of constitutional protections and should be protected by law in terms of religious freedom as well. The point is: there is absolutely no justification for treating graves, human remains, and burial offerings and personal property of Native American's any differently than those of any other group.[53] In 1989, Nebraska passed a law requiring the state to return tribal remains for reburial. Stanford University, the University of Minnesota, Seattle University, and the University of Nebraska are the first universities to step forward and return tribal remains and regalia to their peoples. The Smithsonian has reversed a long-standing policy and agreed to return what does not belong to them as well.

In 1996, USA president Bill Clinton signed an executive order (Eo. 13007) for preservation of sacred sites.

EXECUTIVE ORDER

Indian Sacred Sites

By the authority vested in me as President by the Constitution and the laws of the United States, in furtherance of Federal treaties, and in order to protect and preserve Indian religious practices, it is hereby ordered:

Section 1. *Accommodation of Sacred Sites.* (a) In managing Federal lands, each executive branch agency with statutory or administrative responsibility for the management of Federal lands shall, to the extent practicable, permitted by law, and not clearly inconsistent with essential agency functions, (1) accommodate access to and ceremonial use of Indian sacred sites by Indian religious practitioners and (2) avoid adversely affecting the physical integrity of such sacred sites. Where appropriate, agencies shall maintain the confidentiality of sacred sites.[54]

However, LaDuke (2005) shows us with the example of the Apache and Mt. Graham how USA-imposed rules and laws impact Native American religious freedom, even after Eo. 13007.[55] Mt. Graham is a Holy place. *Dzil nchaa si an*, the chief, the most important sacred mountain, rises 10,700 ft. in the Sonoran Desert. The University of Arizona and the USA military, even the Catholic church and the Pope, have gotten involved in seeking to build an observatory on Mt. Graham. What is supposed to be a project about "pure science" includes military research contracts. Mt. Graham is about money for the USA, but it is about respect for the Apache. The Apache have fought the building of an observatory on Mt. Graham, and now find they are being required by law to seek a permit to pray there.

Another example LaDuke gives us is the Salt Mother, Salt Lake, UT, the source of salt for Zuni, Acoma, Navajo, Apache, and others, for their ceremonial lives. She tells the story of the Peabody Coal's Black Mesa Mine and adjacent Kayenta Mine. The tribal peoples call it the *asabakeshiinh*, the spider that has been feeding off the water and land of the Hopi and Navajo for more than 35 years. Imbedded in the story of the mines is a story of betrayal by John Boyden, whom the tribes trusted to represent them, and how the coal company is draining the watershed in the area (Colorado), that supplies the water for the Black Mesa, and is the Navajo-Aquifer, the sole source of dependable drinking water for the region. Again, tribal peoples are fighting the treating of water as a commodity, and the selling of something sacred. Now there is an added problem as the mines are sources of jobs and incomes ($85 million a year in royalties and spin-offs to the two tribes). After nine years of fighting in White man's courts, 600 acres of the Salt Lake area was transferred back to the Zuni, and the lake was designated a "neutral zone."

Euro-western Americans are starting to understand the damage their ancestors have done to their indigenous neighbors and are helping to give back the land and rebuild the horse herds, the sheep, the salmon, and the corn, for example. One religious group stands out as effective in fighting side by side with the Senecas in New York and the Native Americans in the Pacific Northwest over fishing rights during the 1960s, and that is the Quakers, also known as the American Friends Service Committee.[56] Unitarian Universalists have joined in fighting for indigenous rights more recently.

LaDuke tells us about Klamath land and life on the Klamath River and the wetlands that nourish southern Oregon. She tells us about the Klamath and Modoc tribes, the Yahoosk in band in Snake Paiute, and further downriver the Karuk, Yurok, and Hupa tribes. Recently, they have been restored to tribal status and they have returned to their territory and their fish, the suckerfish. They have retained their water and fishing rights and are able to participate in their ceremonies. There are efforts to remove dams that have been built on the river so that there will be enough water to support the suckerfish and their revival, and the hope is that these efforts will succeed.

LaDuke tells the story of the Navajo's and the slaughter of their sheep, first in 1863 when the army sought to relocate the Navajos to NM territory and slaughtered all but the sheep in remote areas, and second when the USA sought to build Hover Dam during the 1930s and accused the Navajo's of causing too much soil erosion through their sheep grazing practices. Cajete also writes about this painful story. The second time occurred when the USA military came to the Navajo Reservation and carried out government orders for "livestock reduction," which meant the slaughtering of their sheep (their kin). The trauma of witnessing this slaughter is something from which the Navajos still are recovering. From their ontological relational threads in their net, as I describe their spiritual beliefs, they embrace and celebrate the interdependence and importance of all things, including the plants, animals, humans, and Holy People. The Spanish introduced the sheep (Navajo-Churro) to the Navajos in the 1600s, and they adopted them as a gift from the spirits. Having sheep meant that people didn't have to chase game so much. The sheep relied on people for protection, food, and water and people relied on sheep for wealth, clothing, and food. When the sheep were slaughtered in the 1930s, soil erosion increased, instead of decreasing, as it turned out that the Navajos wisely were moving the sheep throughout the Reservation and the sheep were helping to keep plant life thriving that stopped erosion. That plant life changed over time without the sheep there to eat what they had been eating and inedible weeds took over that do not protect the land. There are efforts today to revive the ancient sheep stock, saving them from extinction, and to recover the native plants and land.[57]

LaDuke tells us Euro-western and Native Americans are working together to bring back the horses and the land in the Wallowa Valley, in Idaho. The Nez Perce peoples are famous for their horses, which are called Appaloosa. Their land historically was western Washington and Oregon and Idaho (13.5 million acres), where the Umatilla, Yakama, Cayuse, Palous, and Walla Walla peoples lived. Additionally, in the Great Lakes region, the Namewag are seeking to bring back the sturgeon and people to the area. Natives are running hatcheries and rebuilding the sturgeon population. They are also getting dams taken down, and building sloping rapids that are more fish friendly. The efforts include cleaning up the rivers (hauling away the garbage), and protecting the plants and animals from chemical and social destruction. At Pine Ridge Reservation in South Dakota, home of the Lakota, they are harvesting the wind as an alternative, Earth friendly energy source. The wind is *wakan*, a Holy, great power.

In terms of recovery work involving plants, LaDuke tells us about the Anishinaabeg peoples' efforts to reclaim wild rice in the Minnesota 6,000 lakes area. The rice crops have been affected by water levels in the lakes, toxic contamination, and the dams. The seeds cannot germinate, as the silt at the bottom of the lakes is too thick. Plant recovery work has to address huge conflicts of worldviews over: whose plant is this? Seed companies such as Monsanto have sought to claim ownership over the wild rice and white corn, both of which are "cross-pollinators" central to the tribal peoples rituals and lives. Daybreak Farm and Food Project seeks to revitalize Iroquois white corn, known as grits in the South. They seek to revive farming traditions and teach these in the schools, connecting these farming traditions to "success" and value in the community. Most celebrations in the Iroquois communities are tied directly or indirectly to agriculture. They are close to the Pueblos in their spiritual beliefs (another agriculturally based tribe). They are the original organic farmers: rotating crops, paying attention to when one plants (to miss insect cycles), and intercropping are all long-time practices in indigenous agricultural practices.

In Chapter 8 of Cajete's collection of essays, *A People's Ecology*, Yvonne Dion-Buffalo and John Mohawk write about white corn recovery efforts in "Daybreak Farm and Food Project Seeks Revitalization of White Corn Usage."58 They discuss the history of traditional foods, tamalli, made with a masa dough (corn), and what the Spanish brought (pigs, a rich culinary tradition of cooking with lard). Americans brought tomatoes, potatoes, many types of beans and squash, peppers, and peanuts. The Great Transformation changed tribal communities from rural to urban, and in that transformation diets changed from traditional foods, that send sugars into the blood stream slowly and over a period of time, to sugars that enter the blood stream quickly. The result for natives has been a surge in health problems such as diabetes.

There are several essays in Cajete's collection that discuss the recovery of traditional foods and medicinal practices with herbs, and efforts to improve diets. It is the real green revolution, as Kenny Ausubel describes in "It is Time to Plant."59 The farmers are trying to encourage biodiversity. Pueblo Indians date back 40,000 years. Recovery of their traditions is a primary source of health and healing. Their knowledge of the plants, for food and medicine, is vast (but getting lost quickly, within two generations). Efforts are going on to recover that knowledge, replant the ancient seeds, and get the native plants growing again. We learn the story of Gabriel Howearth, who began collecting ancient seeds and brought them to plant a biodiversity garden in San Juan Pueblo. He was growing amaranth, and *quinoa*, rare herbs, varieties of tomatoes, peppers, potatoes, chilies, all of which come from indigenous people of the Americas, as well as chocolate, sugar, and tobacco. We learn about Seeds of Change, a Native Scholar Program, a Bioneers Conference, the Collective Heritage Institute, and the Restorative Development Initiative, as examples of efforts to train young growers in ecological farming practices. There is a growing effort to identify plants grown by native farmers as "Native certified" to help with marketing and sales for the farmers. Indigenous farmers are actively seeking a sustainable eco-economy that means: demanding irradiated foods continue to be labeled, insisting organic food standards are rigorous and coherent, and opposing distribution of "terminator technology" (Monsanto Corps, seeds that render plants sterile).[60]

Even in terms of building practices, Paula Baker tells us in Cajete's book that since the 1970s our homes have become so air tight, we are breathing a chemical soup.[61] We need to make our homes breathable, as well as beautiful. We learn about a movement in Europe called "baubiology"—the study of how buildings affect human health. Key concepts in baubiology are interaction and permeability. The basic principles are: use nontoxic materials, consider the site geobiology and preservation of natural magnetic fields, incorporate natural light, illumination, and color, architectural proportion and harmonic order of space (*feng shui*), minimize manufactured electromagnetic fields, respect living arrangements of families and the larger community, and use local and natural materials that are renewable and low in embodied energy (such as Wind, Solar, and Earth). It is recommended that we build our homes with breathing walls such as adobe, cob, rammed earth, straw bale, and straw/clay.

I hope the examples offered in this section help Euro-western Americans begin to understand that from a Native American perspective, today's problems and movements show us the superiority of First Nations traditions. The goal is not to encourage us to return to the past. Cajete (1999) tells us: "I believe that, when the traditionalists realize the basis of Indian tribal religions is not preserving social forms and ceremonies but creating new forms and ceremonies to confront new situations, they will have an extremely promising future."[62] The goal is to learn from our past mistakes, and find ways to move forward together, by mending and reweaving our fishing nets with weft threads of relationality.

Conclusion

When children are born into communities, they are taught how to make sense of their booming, buzzing, aromatic experiences through the language and customs taught to them by their community. This is their ontology, and using my metaphor, it is the weft threads in the fishing net they are given by their kin to help them survive in this great Ocean. Besides their ontological threads of being, these nets also contain warp threads of epistemology (knowing), to help them decide what to leave in and out of their fishing nets. Indigenous children are taught various descriptions from their own kin, such as First Man and First Woman (Dinè) or the Sacred Hoop (the Keres of Laguna Pueblo). These origination stories are gifts from the Great Spirit, that are given to their people in dreams and stories, passed down from generation to generation to help the children weave and reweave their ontological and epistemological nets and learn how to cast them into the water. These nets are alive and what their families catch in their nets are alive as well. The children are taught to be grateful for what their communities' nets offer them in terms of what they are able to catch, and to give thanks for the animals (fish) that give their lives and the plants that become part of the net, as well as feed the animals and help them grow and thrive. They are taught to give thanks for the clothing and shelter the plants and animals offer to the peoples to cover and protect them from harmful exposure.

The children are taught that the Ocean, using my metaphor, is living and full of spirituality, and that those spiritual forces will govern and guide our lives if we are open to them and listen and attend. The children are taught the importance of developing and maintaining a constant relationship with these spiritual forces through their daily practice. They are taught that the Ocean (the Great Spirit) is good, and that what comes from the Ocean is not evil, it is an active force that demands our attention and our participation. They are taught to see everything as connected to everything else, and that this connection is circular in that we begin as part of this unified whole universe, our Ocean, we become separate and distinguishable, but that is only temporary, we will eventually become indistinguishably part of our Ocean again.

The children are taught that their actions affect their community and they need to live their lives with humility, understanding, and respect for the sacredness of their place and all living things on that place (land in my metaphor is the raft/boat upon which the community lives, which comes from the Ocean and goes back to the Ocean over time). They are taught that they have stewardship responsibilities to help maintain their communities' nets and boats and to teach their children how to do the same. They learn how to not bring destruction or harm to their community but instead help to achieve balance and sustainability, and find ways to contribute to the daily spiritual practice of theirs and their communities' lives.

We all come from indigenous tribes, we are all the children of peoples who learned how to survive and thrive on this land, surrounded by our infinite Ocean, our universe. We do not have one way of living, we have many ways: some that are helping to maintain our universe and some that are harming it. As the harm increases and the destruction continues to compound (the pollution, diseases, wars), we are becoming more aware that we are not just harming others; we are harming ourselves. We are making it harder and harder for us to live and are risking even greater harm to our children and grandchildren, and their children too. We owe it to the next three generations, the past three generations, and our own generation to embrace the importance of treating our neighbors and kin with respect and dignity, realizing that we are all fallible human beings who make mistakes and that the universe is larger than any of us can comprehend. None of us have fishing nets fine enough to catch up all that is in our Ocean; much continues to spill out over the top and through the holes of our nets. We can learn from each other and gain in our wisdom and understanding, making it possible for us to continually improve our living while we are afloat. We can learn from each other how to be good stewards of our fishing nets and how to adapt them and improve upon them, or we can disregard what others have learned, destroy their fishing nets, push them to extinction, and watch the quality of our lives continue to decline. The choices are ours to make. There is enough room in this Ocean for all of us, if we reweave our ontological nets with threads of relationality, as I have described here, but there is not going to be room for any of us if we continue the destructive directions in which we have been going.[63]

Notes

1. I use the term "Euro-western" to represent the western views that have their roots in Europe, predominantly Ancient Greece. The early colonists to the Americas came from the continent of Europe, predominantly Spain, Portugal, France, England, and Holland (today's Netherlands).
2. I capitalize tribal names as we would for national identities, to honor their specific cultures, but do not capitalize general group names such as "tribal peoples" or "indigenous

peoples" as a way to emphasize they did/do not make claims to absolute Truth in the ways that Europeans did/do, theirs was and continues to be a more pluralistic view of multiple truths.

3. Maria Lugones, "Playfulness, 'World' Traveling, and Loving Perception," *Hypatia* 2 (Summer 1987): 3–19.
4. Vine Deloria, Jr. *For This Land: Writings on Religion in America*, James Treat (Intro.) (New York and London: Routledge, 1999a).
5. Deloria, Jr., "Is Religion Possible?" 1992, 1999a, p. 261.
6. *Ibid.*, p. 264.
7. *Ibid.*, p. 265, emphasis in original.
8. *Ibid.*, p. 140.
9. *Ibid.*, p. 140.
10. See Chapter 8 of my *Relational "(e)pistemologies"* (New York: Peter Lang, 2003) for an in depth discussion of these scientific examples and more.
11. Steven M. Cahn, *The Philosophical Foundations of Education* (New York: Harper & Row, 1970).
12. Deloria, Jr., *For This Land*, p. 34.
13. Deloria, Jr., *ibid.*, "Reflection and Revelation: Knowing Land, Places and Ourselves," 1991, 1999a, p. 252.
14. *Ibid.*, p. 254–255.
15. *Ibid.*, p. 259.
16. *Ibid.*, p. 260.
17. Deloria, Jr., "Is Religion Possible?" 1992, 1999a, p. 268.
18. *Ibid.*, p. 268.
19. Gregory Cajete, *Look to the Mountain: An Ecology of Indigenous Education* (Durango, CO: Kivakí Press, 1994); Gregory Cajete, *A People's Ecology: Explorations in Sustainable Living* (Santa Fe, NM: Clear Light Publishers, 1999).
20. Cajete, 1999, p. 3.
21. *Ibid.*, p. 6.
22. *Ibid.*, p. 15.
23. Gregory Cajete, *Native Science: Natural Laws of Interdependence* (Santa Fe, NM: Clear Light Publishers, 2000), p. 53.
24. *Ibid.*, p. 5.
25. Winona LaDuke, *Recovering the Sacred: The Power of Naming and Claiming* (Cambridge, MA: South End Press, 2005).
26. Bruce E. Johansen, *Native American Political Systems and the Evolution of Democracy* (Westport, CT: Greenwood Press, 1996); Scott Pratt, *Native Pragmatism: Rethinking the Roots of American Philosophy* (Bloomington, IN: Indiana University Press, 2002).
27. Deloria, Jr., *For This Land*, p. 134.
28. *Ibid.*, p. 129.
29. Deloria, Jr., "On Liberation," 1977, 1999a, p. 106.
30. Ibid., pp. 106–107.
31. Deloria Jr., 1999a, p. 133.
32. LaDuke, *Recovering the Sacred*, 2005.

33. James Treat, "Introduction," *For This Land*, 1999a, p. 6.
34. *Ibid.*
35. *Ibid.*, p. 7.
36. Deloria, Jr., 1999a, p. 51.
37. Barbara J. Thayer-Bacon, *Beyond Liberal Democracy in Schools: The Power of Pluralism* (New York: Teachers College Press, 2008), Chapter 4 in particular.
38. Deloria, Jr., "Christianity and Indigenous Religion. Friends or Enemies?" 1987, 1999a, p. 146.
39. Islam shares the same roots sacred text of the Old Testament, and is commemorative of the life of Mohammed, but it does not have a harmful history with indigenous peoples in the Americas and is not discussed in the sources I read.
40. Deloria, Jr., *For This Land*, 1999a, p. 86.
41. *Ibid.*, p. 148.
42. Deloria, Jr., "An Open Letter to the Heads of the Christian Churches in America," 1972, 1999a, pp. 79–80.
43. Deloria, Jr., *For This Land*, 1999a.
44. *Ibid.*, pp. 34, 56.
45. *Ibid.*, p. 76.
46. James E. Lovelock, *Gaia: A New Look at Life on Earth* (Oxford, New York: Oxford University Press, 1979, 1987).
47. Deloria, Jr., *For This Land*, 1999a, p. 168.
48. *Quick Bear v. Leupp*, 1908, that ruled churches could use tribal lands for their schools; *Rosebud Sioux Tribe v. Kneip* in 1977, 9–0 decision against the tribe concerning Congress's intent to diminish the Reservation boundaries without consent of three fourths of the adult males on the Reservation as required by the original 1889 Treaty; *Lyng v. Northwest Indian Cementery Assn*, 1988, that ruled 5–3 that construction of a road to harvest timber in the Chimney Rock area does not violate the First Amendment regardless of its effect on religious practices; *Oregon v. Smith*, 1990, that determined that the state could deny unemployment benefits to a person fired for violating a state prohibition on the use of peyote, even though the use of the drug was part of a religious ritual. Although states have the *power* to accommodate otherwise illegal acts done in the pursuit of religious beliefs, they are not *required* to do so (Wikipedia, accessed 1/14/2015).
49. Deloria, Jr., *For This Land*, 1999a, p. 204.
50. Deloria, Jr., "Sacred Lands and Religious Freedom," (1991, 1999a).
51. *Ibid.*, p. 211.
52. *Ibid.*, p. 196.
53. *Ibid.*, p. 210.
54. www.nps.gov/history/local-law/eo13007.htm.
55. LaDuke, *Recovering the Sacred*, 2005.
56. Deloria, Jr., 1999a, p. 55.
57. *Between Sacred Mountains: Navajo Stories and Lessons from the Land* (Tucson: Sun Tracks and the University of Arizona Press, 1982, 1994), Lawrence Shorty, "A Navajo's Meditations," Chapter 6, in Gregory Cajete, *A People's Ecology*, 1999.

58. Yvonne Dion-Buffalo, and John Mohawk, "Daybreak Farm and Food Project Seeks Revitalization of White Corn Usage," Chapter 8, in Cajete, *A People's Ecology*, 1999.
59. Kenny Ausubel, "It is Time to Plant," Chapter 3, in Cajete, *A People's Ecology*, 1999.
60. John Macker, "Natural Foods Retailers as Activists for Sustainable Lifestyles," Chapter 13, Cajete, *A People's Ecology*, 1999.
61. Paula Bake, "Renaissance of Ancient Building Practices," Chapter 12, Cajete, *A People's Ecology*, 1999.
62. Cajete, *A People's Ecology*, 1999, p. 42.

· 3 ·

PLANTS: DELEUZE'S AND GUATTARI'S RHIZOMES

Introduction

So far, we have explored relational ontologies in terms of Oceans and fishing nets, with the help of William James's classical pragmatism (radical empiricism) and feminist theories (Introduction, Chapter 1), and First Nations' expressions of relationality in terms of the Land (Chapter 2). This chapter takes a turn to the European continent and considers Gilles Deleuze's and Félix Guattari's rhizomatic model to illustrate a relational ontology. One of the ways Deleuze and Guattari describe rhizomes is in terms of a tension between trees and grasses, which is why their work is placed in a chapter labeled Plants. The tension they describe is between deeply rooted structures, which Deleuze and Guattari refer to as "arboretum or tree models" and more shallow rooted grass-like structures, which they refer to as "rhizomes or plateaus," and I will refer to as crabgrass. If one is from the South, crabgrass is as common as kudzu, but for those not familiar with this type of grass, it is able to withstand a significant amount of heat and sun, turns brown in the winter but withstands cold temperatures well, stays snug to the ground, and it spreads with ease.

Deleuze and Guattari's *A Thousand Plateaus*, a key source here, is a companion volume to *Anti-Oedipus*, and together they make up *Capitalism and*

Schizophrenia.[1] In their book description they assure us it is not necessary to read these books or the essays within them in any particular order; they compare the reading to listening to a record, where one can replay favorites and skip over other selections. Their book is an assemblage, a multiplicity, much like the rhizomatic model that they describe. Their text is open, not the final word, and we will take them at their word.

Deleuze and Guattari discuss the tension between trees and grass in multiple ways in *A Thousand Plateaus*, including between novellas and tales, the smooth and striated, and nomads and the war machine. I would like to illustrate the tension between trees and grasses through a close look at higher education (colleges/universities), as a social institution that can serve as a rich case study of their rhizomatic model, thus extending their theory. I don't want to mend their relational net so much as extend it, so that it's easier to appreciate how it serves as an important example of relational ontologies. Maybe, we will find, we need to do some mending along the way.

I will discuss this tension between trees and grass in higher education in multiple ways too: between long-standing universities and newly opened universities, between different colleges within universities, and between different departments and programs. Long-standing disciplines of study such as history, philosophy, languages (e.g., Latin), mathematics, and the "hard" sciences (i.e., physics, chemistry, and biology) represent tree-like examples and more recent interdisciplinary programs such as women's studies (now often renamed as gender studies), African, Latin, and Native Studies (or renamed as Indigenous or First Nations Studies), and cultural studies represent grass-like examples. The social sciences such as psychology, sociology, and economics are younger than the deep-rooted disciplines, while education seems to enjoy a status similar to business, nursing, or architecture, more professional in model than viewed as a deep-rooted discipline. Of course, this description of education does not necessarily ring true at an international level for there are places where "education" is viewed as a longer standing discipline, such as in Russia, Germany, and possibly China.

I want to explore the pros and cons of grass and trees through my experiences in two very different higher education institutions, one in the United States of America (USA) and another in the European Union (EU). The university in the USA is the University of Tennessee in Knoxville (UTK), where I have been a professor for over 15 years, and the university in the EU is the University of Luxembourg (UniLux), where I was a visiting scholar with my host for one semester.[2] My host and I shared coffee and meals and compared notes on our two universities while he hosted me in the spring, 2014, and he has since left the position he had there in December of 2015. I was never an "insider" to UniLux, so I cannot claim any clear vision of the structure, but I learned while I was there that my host didn't have so clear of a vision of the university's structure either. One observation we have is that the longer a university exists the more tree-like it becomes, in terms of its deeply rooted structure. UTK, young by European standards, is one of the oldest public universities in the USA. Within this deep-rooted university a dean in the college of education was able to acquire significant funding and central administration support, and give the college the opportunity to restructure itself as small units instead of larger departments. As a result of this restructuring, a new unit, Cultural Studies of Education, was born in the mid-1990s, which I joined in 2000. UniLux was founded in 2003, making it one of the newest universities in the EU. My host and I were drawn to work at our different universities due to their interdisciplinary focus within their loose structures, we were attracted to their crabgrass natures, but neither of us have survived in that state of nature due to the lack of protection crabgrass offers given universities' tendencies to create and seek to maintain deeper rooted tree structures.

Deleuze and Guattari tell us in their Introduction: "We are tired of trees [...]. They've made us suffer enough" (loc. 15). My host and I were too, and we sought the excitement of more creative freedom and possibilities for growth and transformation in grass-type places. We went to our institutions not seeking to sow, but to grow offshoots, as Deleuze and Guattari recommend. However, we have gained greater appreciation of trees in the process of our moves to more grass-like spaces as trees can withstand extreme weather conditions such as droughts and storms (deep recessions, changes in administration and faculty) due to their deeper roots and they are more likely to be able to maintain their shape and form, thus offering protection when the weather gets bad. Grass is more dependent on regular sources of moisture (resources such as administrative support, the refilling of faculty lines) and is likely to come and go in unpredictable ways. It also is likely to be eaten by grazing animals. Grass offers little protection, only the knowledge that it will reappear somewhere, somehow, if one is able to wait out the storm or drought (and find a way to survive in the meanwhile).

I begin with a more detailed description of Deleuze and Guattari's rhizomes, and then move to a comparison of the two universities. My aim here is not to resolve the tension between trees and grass, but to explore that tension and demonstrate its rich application to higher education. My claim is that Deleuze and Guattari's rhizomatic model can serve as an excellent example of a relational ontology. I will make that claim clearer by the end of this chapter.

Rhizomes (or Plateaus)

Deleuze and Guattari describe rhizomes in their Introduction to *A Thousand Plateaus*. A rhizome, according to my desktop dictionary, is literally a botanic term for a root-like horizontal stem that grows under or along the ground and send out roots from its lower surface and leaves or shoots from its upper surface. Deleuze and Guattari mean for their description to include the best and worse about rhizomes and to be an approximation of characteristics. As I describe rhizomes, please think about crabgrass. "(A)ny point of a rhizome can be connected to anything other, and must be" (loc. 7). However, "not every trait in a rhizome is necessarily linked to a linguistic feature" (loc. 7). These are principles 1 and 2: *connection* and *heterogeneity*. A rhizome ceaselessly establishes connections but at the same time it is never closed, it can never be completely analyzed. Language analyzed in search of roots is genealogical, but a rhizomatic type of method of analysis of language can only do so by decentering it (loc. 8). Principle 3: *multiplicity*: there are no points or positions in a rhizome, only lines (loc. 8). All multiplicities are flat; we speak of "a *plane of consistency* of multiplicities. [...] Multiplicities are defined by the outside [...] *Flat multiplicities of n dimensions* are a signifying and a subjective. They are designated by indefinite articles [...]" (loc. 9, emphasis in original). *Some* crabgrass. Principle 4: *a signifying rupture*. You can break a rhizome but it will start up again on one of its old lines or on new lines.

Deleuze and Guattari compare rhizomes to ants, that we can never get rid of, and viruses, but crabgrass works fine here as an example, for even if one manages to pull it all out of one's yard, which is next to impossible to do as the roots continually break and then reform themselves, the seeds of the grass will blow over to one's yard from the neighbor's lawn or the nearby field, and crabgrass will be back in that formerly cleared yard in no time at all. "The rhizome is an antigenealogy" (loc. 11). Principles 5 and 6: *cartography* and *decalcomania*: "a rhizome is not amenable to any structural or generative model. It is a stranger to any idea of genetic axis or deep structure" (loc. 12). While tree logic is a logic tracing and reproduction, rhizomatic logic is "*a map and not a tracing*" (loc. 12, emphasis in original). It always has multiple entryways. It can be viewed from many angles and has to do with performance. Desire always moves and produces by rhizome (loc. 14).

In summary: a rhizome connects any point to any other point; it is never reducible to the one nor the multiple; it is not composed of units but rather directions in motion; it is always in the middle; it is made only of lines of segmentarity and stratification, lines of flight or deterritorialization; it is not the object of reproduction; it is an antigenealogy, a short-term or antimemory; it operates by variation, expansion, conquest, capture, offshoot; it is tracings that must be put on a map; it's an acentered, nonhierarchical, nonsignifying system without a general and without an organizing memory; it is made of plateaus (loc. 21). "The tree imposes the verb 'to be,' but the fabric of the rhizome is the conjunction, 'and [...] and [...] and [...]'" (loc. 25).

Universities as Trees

In various countries around the world we can find colleges and universities that have been in existence for hundreds of years. The University of Bologna, in Italy, was founded in 1088, the University of Paris, France was founded between 1160 and 1250, the University of Oxford was founded in 1096–1167, and New College, in Oxford, England (now UK) was founded in 1379, for example. Scotland's oldest university, the University of Edinburgh, was founded in 1583, and Japan's University of Tokyo began as a private college of Confucian studies in 1630. In Latin America, the Universidad Michoacana de San Nicolás Obispa (St. Nicholas Bishop College) was founded in Mexico in 1540 by King Carlos I of Spain. The National University of San Marcos, in Lima, Peru was founded in 1551, as well as Mexico's second oldest university, known now as the National Autonomous University of Mexico. Columbia's oldest university is Saint Thomas Aquinas University, founded in 1580, and Argentina's oldest is National University of Córdoba, 1613. In the USA, Harvard University is the oldest, located in Cambridge, Massachusetts, founded in 1636 and chartered in 1650.

I work at a university in the USA that is in the state of Tennessee and was founded in 1794 as Blount College by Rev. Samuel Carrick, two years prior to the state becoming a state, making it one of the USA's oldest colleges, but still 600+ years younger than New College in Oxford.[3] Blount College is now known as the University of Tennessee, but it has changed its name three times, prior to becoming the University of Tennessee. My home is located downtown on the same place where the college was originally located when it was called Blount College, named after the governor of the southwest territory at the time, who donated the land for the college. There is a historical plaque on my building that marks the location as where the University of Tennessee began as Blount College.

When we research the history of some of the world's oldest universities with the deepest roots, we find that they were not easy to found and their beginnings often are marked by fits and starts, times when they had to close down, and times when they had to move their locations and restart under new names. The University of Tennessee experienced fits and starts too, closing down twice and changing names three times before becoming the University of Tennessee. The first time it closed down was due to the loss of funding when the first president (and only faculty member), Rev. Samuel Carrick, died in 1809. He is buried in the church graveyard right behind my building, since he also served as the church's pastor, although Blount College was a nonsectarian college, rare for a college from that time period. Carrick's death closed down Blount College for a decade, until it could secure more funds through a temporary partnership with a boys' school. When it reopened in 1820 it had a new name, East Tennessee College. It had six faculty and around 95 students. East Tennessee College moved from its original downtown location to "the hill" when it dissolved its partnership with the boys' school in 1826, and this is where it has stayed and grown significantly in its 220+ years.

The second time UTK closed down was due to the Civil War, when it became a hospital for the Confederate Army, and later for Union troops. When it reopened after the Civil War in 1866, after much repair work due to damage from the war, it was renamed East Tennessee University. It became the University of Tennessee in 1879. Today, as the flagship university for the state, the University of Tennessee has an enrollment of 27,000+ and a faculty of 1,500+. As we can see from my description, UTK was not always stable and durable as an arboretum structure but it has become so over time.

Trees are not easy to plant and succeed in having them take root, and even after they take root they are not easy to relocate without risking harming the tree. Their roots take hold and dig down deeply into the ground, so that they can grow tall and thrive, and digging up those roots is not only difficult but attempting to do so can damage the roots and kill the tree. On the plus side, a deeply rooted tree can withstand strong winds, droughts and floods, even fire, and survive. It is able to find nourishment deep within the ground and use its leaves for protection as well as for making food to sustain itself.

History gives trees their strength, and in universities this history comes in the form of: longstanding good reputations built on the outstanding work of their faculty and the success of their alumni; strong financial foundations built on endowments and alumni giving over the years, earnings generated through royalties from their research and student tuitions; and significant amounts of evidence that they are able to contribute back to their local communities and state economies, and even federal government needs (UTK contributes significantly to the USA's defense and energy programs, for example).

Because of its long-established reputation and history, UTK does not have to worry about its survival when the state's economy gets tight in current times. As the state's flagship university, it is the last university to face cuts in funding and the first to get more funding as it becomes available. It may face years of status quo, even years where it has to prune branches, but the pruning is done to maintain the health of the tree. UTK has the highest demand for the most qualified students in the state and applications tend to go up when the economy goes down, as students enroll to help them seek other job possibilities. It has the highest paid faculty in the state system and a strong base of stability with a significant number of faculty who work there for many years. Its most successful alumni make sure its needs are met as it represents the best the state has to offer, and they need UTK to succeed for businesses and families to be drawn to living and working in the state. All of these are strong positives on behalf of trees. If one is fortunate enough to be offered a job at UTK and to earn tenure, one can feel pretty assured their job will continue to exist. They may have to adapt their research and teaching to the needs of the university as conditions change, but they will be given the opportunity to adapt.

However, because of trees' deep-rootedness, they are difficult to change. They become more conservative places, as their traditions and rituals grow. Their size alone makes changes difficult, and their policies put in place to help them function smoothly and protect them also serve as barriers that make it difficult to reform their programs, departments, schools, and colleges within. The longer faculty work at UTK, the more they have invested in the structures they have helped to build and the more committed they become to "the way things are." They become less willing to change and as they gain in seniority, they also gain power and their voices hold more sway in decisions regarding the future of programs within the university. Senior faculty become the administrators for the university and the chairs for search committees that hire new faculty. It is easy to see how universities become like trees. Even students help in this process, for students grow found of the dormitory that they lived in and don't want to see it replaced by a new structure, and they grow loyal to the programs, departments, schools, and colleges where they obtained their degrees.

Universities as Crabgrass

How do universities make changes? How does crabgrass grow amongst the deeply rooted trees? How does a new university launch itself, beginning as crabgrass as it plants its young roots in the ground, such as UniLux? In the UniLux case, it was launched by government initiative. I will turn to UniLux next, as it is so rare to be able to experience a new university in current times, but let me stay with the University of Tennessee for now as it offers a unique example as well. Often significant changes at already existing universities come in the form of the hiring of a new dean, and/or university president, with support reaching as high as the governor of the state's office. The conditions for change are top down, rather than bottom up ones initiated by faculty. In the case of UTK, a new dean was hired in the mid-1980s (Richard Wisniewski), and he came to UTK as a "change agent" for the college, hired during a time when the former governor of the state, Lamar Alexander, one of the authors of *A Nation At Risk*, was president of the university (1988–1991).[4] Wisniewski was dean until 1996, when he began his phased retirement.

The first reform the College of Education tackled under Dean Wisniewski's leadership was becoming a Holmes Group model for teacher education, changing from a four-year undergraduate degree program, traditional at the time, to a "more rigorous" five-year teacher education program that requires a bachelor's degree from a college of arts and sciences in a specific field of study, such as history, English, or mathematics.[5] Increasing the requirements to become a teacher was one of the recommendations of *A Nation At Risk*. With the Holmes Group model of teacher education, students wanting teaching credentials begin taking education courses during their senior year, and continue with summer courses while they intern in schools in the area during their fifth year. When they complete their teaching credential requirements they are close to having a masters degree in education, and more than 90 percent of them go on to earn their masters degree in the teacher education department at UTK.

Changes related to this fifth-year model of teacher education included designing a new admissions process and reducing redundancies in methods courses. The change was completed by 1990 and the Holmes Group model is still in place at UTK, although more changes have occurred since then. For example, the college has gone back to offering an undergraduate teaching credential for students interested in teaching math and science as the state has a shortage in teachers for those subject areas. In another change, teacher education students no longer take any "educational foundations" courses as requirements toward their credential, whereas during the 1980s and 1990s students had nine quarter hours (when UTK was on a quarter system), which had become a single two-credit semester course in educational foundations by the time I arrived in 2000. Faculty opposed to this fifth-year model warned that the college would lose student applications but that fear has turned out to be unfounded. The college has increased in number and quality of student applicants, in terms of students' grade-point averages, with the fifth-year model and the reputation of quality of teachers graduating from UTK has also grown with the addition of a full-year internship in schools.

Dean Wisniewski's success in changing the College of Education's teacher education program from an undergraduate to a graduate program helped him gain support for his next reform efforts, for he was not finished as a change agent at UTK with the reform efforts in teacher education. With the help of the university system president who was also a past two-term governor of the state, Lamar Alexander, Wisniewski was able to obtain a half-million dollar grant from a foundation, Philip Morris Companies (also Kraft Foods), based on a proposal for remodeling the College of Education into the New College of Education. The dean did not have a preconceived structural plan for the college, the most prevalent rumor among the faculty; however, he did have a strong commitment to the value in the college staying flexible and adaptive to change. From my perspective, he represents a rhizomatic approach to the running of a college, unusual for a dean. In fact, there is a national award for educational reform named after Richard Wisniewski. His motivation to encourage change in the college was not due to external reasons such as financial concerns, nor by order from higher administration. Faculty positions were secure. The goal was to encourage more collaboration across disciplinary lines with the faculty and students within the college. The goal was rhizomatic: to encourage variation, creative adaption, and expansion, to create a nonhierarchical, a centered system that makes connections and brings together diverse scholars emphasizing multidisciplines and conjunctions: and [...] and [...] and.

The first step taken by the dean was to change the college's organization structure, thinking that program changes would follow suit. Dean Wisniewski dissolved *all* seven departments within the college, and those departments resistant to this dissolution ended up opting to leave the college and joined the College of Human Ecology.[6] All of the faculty were encouraged to form new "units" with others in the college with whom they would like to work and were given three years to do this restructuring.[7] They developed alignments based upon various connections they were able to establish with others: some through their research interests, shared philosophies of education, or even just because they were friends and thought they would enjoy working together (although they had to make their case for coming together on some other grounds, but hindsight has revealed those grounds were not enough to hold the unit together once the friends retired).

A faculty coordinator for the organization process was appointed, someone perceived to be fair and balanced as a leader, and faculty members headed the committees formed to begin designing the framework for change. Each year of the reform process a different faculty member was coordinator. The faculty had retreats, held forums, invited guest speakers, visited other reform-minded colleges, circulated newsletters and memos, were invited to small-group breakfast meetings, and eventually composed themselves into 11 units and agreed upon a mission for the New College, all within the first year (1991–1992). The second year they worked on refining the first year's work and creating a New College Planning Document. Throughout this process there were plenty of naysayers and they employed stalling tactics. However, by the end of the second year the Faculty Council held a secret ballot vote and to everyone's surprise, especially the naysayers, they learned that 74 percent of the faculty supported the New College proposal. The third year was spent seeking campus administrative approval, and approval from the Board of Trustees, which they succeeded in achieving after more than 20 faculty met with the university's chancellor and vice chancellor and voiced their strong support for the New College. The university trustees voted unanimously for approval of the New College (July 1, 1994).

This innovative dean of the New College of Education at UTK, Dean Wisniewski, joined the Cultural Studies of Education (CSE) unit during his phase-out years to retirement, as he was a sociologist of education with a research interest in higher education reform. The faculty who formed CSE included people who taught history, philosophy, anthropology, and sociology of education, and people who taught history, philosophy, psychology, and sociology of sport, or what we could describe as the educational studies and sports studies faculty. When they first formed a unit they included three faculty members from Human Services and a faculty member in adolescent literature. The chair of the Faculty Council during the third year of restructuring was also a member of this group, Joan Paul, and she describes it as "perhaps the most diverse of the new college units."[8] During their year of exploring possible unit configurations, the CSE faculty discovered that their research work focused around "culture," in particular power issues and how theory connected to practice, relying on pragmatism and critical theory for their analysis. They came together over concerns for how race, class, gender, and sexual orientation issues were problematic for students in schools as well as student athletes in gyms and on the playing field or court. The faculty developed and began to offer the first Ph.D. in CSE in the country, according to the search committee that hired me in 2000. Their program became a model for others in the USA.

The unit, CSE, created a consensus model for faculty governance, and all faculty in the unit committed to attending the CSE seminar together along with the educational studies and sports studies graduate students. They set up team-teaching models and individuals from educational studies as well as sports studies co-taught a course on social justice, or a research methodology course such as historiography. Joan Paul, a sport historian, was the first unit leader and then when she retired from her administrative post, the faculty in CSE unanimously selected Joy DeSensi to be their unit leader, a much respected and beloved sports sociologist. Joy DeSensi was the unit leader (department head by 2000) who hired me, and Joan Paul and Clint Allison, two historians, served on the search committee, while Bill Morgan, a sport philosopher, chaired the search committee. The educational studies faculty agreed to move their offices over to the Health, Physical Education, and Recreation (HPER) building where the sports studies faculty resided so that they would be near each other and find it easier to work together. That agreement came after a year of discussion. When I joined CSE my office was in a building that feels like a gym and my first office now serves as a storage room (no window); my second office did have a window and looked out on the track. Contrary to anything I have experienced prior or since, the faculty agreed to a faculty evaluation system that required them to all read each other's annual materials and give each other positive and constructive feedback. Faculty took turns taking notes and writing the evaluation letters for each other. If anyone had problems or concerns, those were brought to a unit faculty meeting and openly shared and discussed. As much as possible the administrating of the unit was open and by consensus.

This program's exciting, innovative, creative energy drew five other faculty members over a five-plus-year period of time to work in the CSE unit, including both educational and sports studies faculty. Working under this kind of model felt very supportive and nurturing and I learned a great deal from my diverse colleagues and the students in our unit. At its peak, CSE had ten faculty members in the unit with other faculty on campus affiliated as adjunct faculty. Students were flocking to this exciting, innovative, creative program and they were bringing a CSE influence to their various discipline bases as they were finding jobs that sought a CSE focus. In hindsight, though, the flocking was more with sports studies students than educational studies students because the educational studies students were confused by the degree and thought it required them to take sports courses, while the sports studies students already saw themselves as interested in educational courses as they were getting degrees with an education major.[9] For the educational studies students, having the unit leader be a sports studies faculty member, the faculty offices in the HPER building, and their courses over there too added to their concern about how deep was the connection to sports? For those brave enough to trek over to the HPER building, they found a warm, welcoming atmosphere with scholars excited about the rich connections and relationships they were developing. It truly was a learning community.

Unfortunately, the build up to the peak for New College and CSE in particular was about five years (1994–1999), and it took three years after Dean Wisniewski returned to the faculty in 1996 (and left once his phased-out retirement ended) to lose the unit model and move back to departments (units did not fit into the university's structural norms). An interim dean with 16 years of experience working for Dean Wisniewski replaced Wisniewski while they did a national search for a new dean, only to have their search shut down near completion due to an unanticipated hiring freeze imposed by the state that year. In 1998, a second search for a dean of education also ended unexpectedly when the prime candidate for the position turned them down. Interim Dean Rowell was offered a three-year contract to be Dean Rowell, which he accepted. He was told by the new university president/central administration that he must return the college to having departments, as "units" did not fit the university's structure. Tree logic began to prevail.

The result for the CSE unit was the pushing back together of two units of people who didn't want to be together. In his Afterword, Wisniewski compares what happened to the faculty in the college who took risks and joined with new configurations of colleagues as like a married couple that had decided to get divorced, and found a new, healthier relationship that they committed to, only to find their new marriage annulled and being told they had to return to their original, unhealthy marriage.[10] The metaphor is very telling and a fair description of what happened. I arrived at UTK after that first year of forced return to original marriage, with the educational leadership unit loudly voicing their complaints to central administration, going right over the dean's head in terms of protocol. Within another five years the contentious department was dissolved when central administration got tired of their complaining and the opportunity arose to take action. Faculty were dispersed to various departments, with the sports studies group going back to their home base of exercise science and sports management, and the educational studies faculty not sure where to go. The three of us were all newer faculty with no previous history with UTK's old College of Education model. We had two weeks to decide on one of three departments, with no one to guide us, as our senior educational studies faculty had retired or left the university by then. We chose poorly. Once we chose, we lived with our choice, even after we learned it was the wrong one, for we were trying to protect our junior faculty through the tenure process. Within seven years we lost that department, the junior faculty member didn't earn tenure, and one of us left the university for another university with an outstanding offer of support and the promise of a better place to grow.

Besides not being able to replace Dean Wisniewski when he stepped down with another strong national hire, due to the fiscal crisis the state found itself in, the university's hiring freeze affected faculty hires as well. In his "Afterword," Wisniewski tells us that the dean's office had been holding on to faculty lines as people retired so that they could be used for new faculty hires once the New College was firmly in place. The idea was that all resources would go to supporting the mission of New College and all hires would be faculty who supported that mission as well. When the late 1990s fiscal crisis hit UTK, "all of the empty faculty lines that had been preserved during the planning process were 'swept' or eliminated."[11]

Funding in the state for UTK grew even tighter during the 2000s and the departments that had left the college were collapsed back into the old College of Education, with a new name (College of Education, Health, and Human Sciences) and another interim dean, to save money. The college did have the opportunity to do a national search and hire a new dean in 2004,

Dean Bob Rider, but under the mission of the College of Education, Health, and Human Sciences, not New College's mission. By 2004, New College was gone. Another ten years, and smaller departments have been collapsed into other departments, again to save money, and there is now only one person left as a fulltime tenure-track faculty member in educational studies from the former CSE unit, which is no longer its own program due to its size, but is still offering a concentration area and a certificate under an Education major (which currently is under review for possible revision and deletion as well). Students are still drawn to the CSE courses being offered, and they are able to use their CSE certificates to help them find jobs with a social-justice focus, but the jobs they find in higher education are in discipline bases, or generalized positions.

What happened to this creative, antidisciplinary, multidisciplinary program with its focus on multiplicity, variation, deterritorialization, expansion, and its acentered, nonhierarchical structures? It made rich connections to multiple fields of study, but had none of its own. Faculty in the college could not understand what CSE was as it resisted defining itself, and they were offended by its strong claim to a social justice focus as they thought they cared about social justice too. They liked its efforts to connect theory to practice, but could not understand the very abstract language cultural studies scholars insist on using. When UTK's innovative dean left and the senior faculty in CSE retired, the CSE program was no longer protected. The faculty had grown to resent this perceived dean-favored program so that they did little to help protect it. The university's role, in seeking to maintain its tree structure, was to order the entire crabgrass-like college back into the tree's structure and to appoint an interim dean who would do what central administration requested to make sure the college complied.

All of these changes required faculty to do continual program re/development and service work, which caused some senior faculty to leave UTK for other universities or opt for retirement. What started out as invigorating, exciting work became exhausting, stressful work, as all changes tend to be. Some faculty even became ill and passed away. Younger non-tenured faculty found it difficult to withstand the strife as they tried to be good team players and help with program re/development, while also establishing their own research agendas, and consequently many were not able to publish enough to be rewarded tenure.

As funding in the state dried up with the USA entering the first recession period in the late 1990s, and then a deep recession in 2008, faculty lines were not refilled in an effort to protect the tree's structure, causing the college to lose not only the frozen lines in the late 1990s, but a dozen lines during the 2008–2012 recession as well. Faculty who had once been willing to serve as adjunct faculty to the CSE program pulled back into their discipline bases for protection during the first financial downturn, as the need for assistance rose in their home bases. Key sports studies faculty tucked back into their home bases as well, leaving three educational studies faculty left to find a home; with one of them leaving shortly for another university and another not receiving tenure, that has left one, me. Tragically, the loss of CSE at UTK has become the loss of educational foundations at UTK as well. Thus, UTK serves as an excellent example of the dangers of rhizomatic models in higher education.

Rhizomatic models are creative, enriching places to work, for their flexibility, multiplicity, and interdisciplinarity qualities help students and faculty explore connections and enlarge their thinking. However, without regular watering (administrative and faculty support), they lose ground and begin to dry up. They become easy to pull up and remove. As the lone tenure-track faculty member left still trying to keep CSE courses alive at UTK, I can take heart in knowing that it is impossible to get rid of crabgrass; it hides and its creative forces help it find other ways to reappear, and hopefully begin to thrive again. Right now CSE courses are surviving as a certificate option, a cognate, and a concentration area, and students are still seeking out those courses for their focus on social-justice issues. However, educational studies courses are not being sought as electives for students majoring in various educational degrees anymore as students have required courses within their various programs they must take and these requirements have multiplied over the past decade. As a result, with low student numbers and high need for replacing faculty in more demand areas, the educational studies faculty who left have not been replaced. Sports studies faculty have done a better job of surviving and being replaced as they have retired, but remember, they never moved from their home base in terms of their location, and they were able to slide back into their former department structure easily. Their student numbers never dropped and had to be recovered.

The moral of the University of Tennessee New College of Education, and CSE program/unit stories seems to be: universities need both, grass to help them be adaptive and welcome change, and trees to help them withstand severe weather conditions (droughts, storms, such as recessions and cultural censorship). Wisniewski ends his "Afterword" by saying "New College was not a mistake. It was an attempt to get it right."[12] The tree structure at UTK insisted on departments instead of units in order to meet university policy requirements for representation on university-wide committees, for example. The central administrators also insisted on courses fitting in standard time slots so that classroom assignments can be made and conflicts do not occur. They insisted that courses begin and end in sync with the university-wide school calendar, all of which worked to undermine the growth of New College's crabgrass. However, the loosening of the College of Education's structure and the transformation of the faculty culture that New College achieved, even for a short while, has left the college with a flexibility and adaptability I have never known to exist in other universities of this size, with this much history. This flexibility and adaptability that it lacked before helped the college find ways to survive and even thrive during the next wave of financial crisis the state and university faced.

In hindsight, I am surprised that the College of Education and CSE program were able to hire me in 2000. I am not sure whether I would accept an offer to join another cultural studies unit, knowing how difficult it is to maintain such a tenuous grass-like position within an arboretum structure. Remember, grass is made only of lines of segmentarity and stratification, lines of flight or deterritorialization. I arrived to a college with low faculty morale, and it is only now with the research I have done for this chapter that I have a greater understanding of why. Remember, grass is not the object of reproduction; it is antigenealogy, a short-term or antimemory. It is without a General and without an organizing memory. Working at UTK has ended up being a lonely lesson in rhizomes. I miss my CSE colleagues. The experience has definitely taught me how to be an adaptive survivor. Let's turn to an examination of UniLux as another case study of the tensions between trees and crabgrass.

Luxembourg and the University of Luxembourg

Luxembourg is a small, landlocked country in Western Europe, surrounded by Germany, France, and Belgium.[13] It is officially known as the Grand Duchy of Luxembourg and is the only remaining grand duchy in the world. Luxembourg is less than 1,000 square miles in size (2.586 square kilometers), making it one of the smallest countries in Europe, and its population size is around half a million. Still, it is one of the wealthiest countries in the world, ranked by the United Nations in 2014 to have the world's highest GDP per capita. It is the home to close to 90 banks and is considered a tax haven for the wealthy, ranked second behind Switzerland. The current president of the EU's European Council (EC) is from Luxembourg, and the country was one of the founding members of the EU. Luxembourg is the site of many vital institutions in the EU, such as the European Court of Justice and the European Court of Auditors. The Secretariat of the European Parliament is located in Luxembourg as well.

Luxembourg has a unique, complicated history due to its central location in Western Europe and due to the fact that geographically Luxembourg Castle is protected on Bock rock. It has strategic value and has been taken over by all the countries that surround it at various times throughout its history. This has created a country that is a fusion of Romanic and Germanic Europe, is predominantly Roman Catholic in religious expression, and is trilingual, with Luxembourgish, French, and German all recognized as official languages. French is the preferred language of the government and all official legislation must be conducted in French, but the education system in the country teaches all three languages: Luxembourgish in primary school, German in lower secondary school, and French in higher secondary school. To officially graduate from secondary school, students must be proficient in all three languages, and to be hired as a teacher in Luxembourg one must be proficient in all three languages as well. Salaries are very high for teachers but the job pool is small, as few know Luxembourgish beyond the citizens of Luxembourg. English is also taught in compulsory schools. This makes Luxembourg a unique country for educational research if one wants to explore the pros and cons to schooling that is conducted in multiple languages.

Luxembourg used to be a significant contributor to the steel industry in Western Europe, which began while it was a part of Prussia, but as the steel industry has waned since the 1960s, the country has worked to diversify its industries, focusing particularly on banking and financing. The recent worldwide economic downturns and the role of the banks in the resulting global deep recession have caused Luxembourg to consider more ways to diversify its economy. One form of diversification they have chosen is developing "the business of higher education." The government of Luxembourg founded its only university, the UniLux, in August, 2003.

Before 2003, Luxembourgish students had to leave their country to finish their studies beyond one or two years of postsecondary schooling. For university studies they usually enrolled in Belgium, France, Germany, Austria, and the United Kingdom. The hope is that this new university will allow local citizens of Luxembourg to stay closer to home (although, admittedly, Germany, France, and Belgium are all only about 15 to 30 minutes away, depending on means of travel). They also hope that the country's multilingual education system will attract students and faculty to the university. All courses at UniLux are offered in two languages such as French/English, French/German, and English/German. The university was still in the process of building a new campus when I was there as a visiting scholar, and they were hoping to begin moving in 2015. My description of the university is based on my time in country, spring semester, 2014. It is important to remember my description is from an outsider's perspective, not as a hired member of the faculty, but instead as a guest visitor.

Because of its youth, the university has not had time to develop much in the way of a tree structure. It is very grass-like, including the fact that it is spread between multiple locations. When I was there, the faculty doing educational research were located in Walferdange (in a former castle, including the horse stable), along with the faculty of language and literature, humanities, and arts. My housing was located across the street from Limpertsberg campus, where the faculties of science, technology, and communication, as well as the central administration units were located. My apartment was in a former nunnery which UniLux purchased for university housing. There was a third campus, Kirchberg, which hosted faculty of law, economics, and finance. For me to get to Walferdange from Limpertsberg meant catching a bus into the city center and then catching another bus out to Walferdange, which could take anywhere from 30 to 60 minutes depending on my timing of the buses. The bus into city center ran almost continually but the one out to Walferdange only ran a couple times/hour. When I first arrived to Luxembourg, the day I checked into the Limpertsberg central administration offices and received my apartment key, I also had to find my way out to the mall to shop for bedding and linens, dishes, etc., that I would need in order to live in the apartment and be able to sleep that night. The bus trip to the mall took me past another campus where finance and economics is located. The campus began to feel "spread out" and grassy on day one for me.[14]

Added to an experience of a university located on three campuses, was the way each campus was arranged. When I arrived to the Walferdange campus on my first day there, I asked people walking on the campus if they could point me to the "education building." After several unsuccessful tries, I found an education student who was able to explain to me that there was no "education building." Even at my writing of this chapter I still assumed there must be "education faculty" that I was just never able to find; however, my host has informed me that there were no "education faculty;" there were faculty in the arts and humanities, literature and language, and education (known as FLSHASE) and amongst those faculty there were some whose work focused on education.[15] The "education faculty," as I arrived describing them, were spread between several buildings, and on multiple floors within those various buildings, along with other faculty in the arts and humanities, and literature and language. This made it difficult for me to know where to look for faculty whose work focused on education, their students, or staff. Again, it felt very grass-like. Hopefully, being spread around amongst various buildings helped the faculty find it easier to collaborate with each other. From my perspective, it appeared that there were no tree-like structures built up between the various fields of study in education as well as between the humanities and education that would inhibit their interaction. I understand that the faculty members are encouraged to associate with multiple teams of scholars within the college of FLSHASE. As an outsider to the system, I found the lack of physical structure confusing, and it affected my ability to actually meet most of the faculty whose work focused on education. Apparently, I was looking for something that did not exist.

In the building where I was assigned a shared office with another visiting scholar, a doctoral student from a university in Italy, our common host had his office across the hall. Our host's staff took care of us while we were there, but I never met her/them. I also never received a key to the office I was assigned, nor access to any office equipment such as a printer or the copy machine. Maybe this was due to the short time I was there, or for security reasons? Having had a previous sabbatical as a visiting scholar at Teachers College, Columbia University (TC), where office space is very tight, I was thrilled to have office space. I know how precious those spaces can be in the USA. However, I struggled with feeling disconnected from the faculty during my time at UniLux, as I only managed to meet two other faculty members in the course of six weeks. In fact, I can only claim to have met three faculty members in the course of my entire time in residence in Luxembourg. I began to notice that tree-like structures offer more in my home university and that I was missing these at UniLux.

One of the issues that affect the university and those who work and attend there has to do with the cost of living in Luxembourg. As described previously, Luxembourg is not a large country geographically yet it is a very wealthy country. This translates into Luxembourg being an expensive place to live. Fortunately for my partner and me, the university was able to offer us international student housing, unlike our previous experience at TC. Without that option, we would have probably had to live in Germany, France, or Belgium, as many of the students do, and commute in, because housing is more affordable outside the country, and transportation is excellent, reliable, and affordable. As I checked in at the housing office I listened to students discussing going to Belgium to the nearest IKEA to get their housing supplies, only 15 to 30 minutes away, thus reminding me that I was in a small country and needed to stop thinking in terms of country borders and boundaries, as these were easily crossed. While some borders were easily crossed, such as country boundaries, others were not, such as access to buildings in the evening. I learned that I could not access the Limpertsberg library in the evenings when I was back to my apartment as the buildings were locked after daytime working hours and a security key was needed to get into any building on campus in the evening. I never received a key to my office, the same key that would have let me into the library in the evenings. In fact, my partner and I shared one key between us for our apartment too; keys were not readily available.

Added to the cost of living and size of the country that makes commuting from surrounding countries easy for students, the newness of the university faculty and the flexibility of teaching schedules means that a significant number of the faculty are commuting to UniLux as well. The faculty I did have the chance to meet live as far away as Munich, Germany and I understand others live in the surrounding countries, including the United Kingdom. Much of their work they can do via email, and they may need to come to campus only biweekly for seminars and/or other meetings, so it is easier to commute then to uproot their families from their home bases. I found that there were days when I would show up to my office on the Walferdange campus and set off the motion lights in the hallway of my building, as I appeared to be the first one there, arriving around nine to ten am. That was a surprise! As there were people in offices, and administrators were keeping regular hours, I'm not sure if they hadn't been in the halls for awhile, or if the administrators' offices were not in my building? Again, the experience felt decentering, connected and not, with multiple entryways but no one there when I entered. Strange! This caused me to reflect more on the value of tree-like structures.

There is one more story I want to tell which affected my entire time in Luxembourg and again is due to UniLux's youth, and lack of arboretum structure, from my perspective. In order for me to live in Luxembourg for an entire semester, I would need a working visa. Tourist visas are only good for 90 days of travel in the EU. According to the UniLux website, classes begin in mid-February and end in May, with exams in the month of June. We planned to leave UTK the beginning of January and travel for six weeks prior to arriving in Luxembourg in mid-February to avoid the cold and the housing cost. We planned to live in Luxembourg for the semester, taking weekend trips, and then travel again in the summer after the semester ended. We gave up our home for January to August, when my sabbatical would end. This plan was based on tree logic, but UniLux is rhizomatic, operating much more like crabgrass than trees.

My paperwork for my working visa was not filed in September when I submitted it to UniLux, but instead in December. That was too late to receive a work visa, as it takes three months to process. Why it was late seemed to be related to UniLux not having developed a clear protocol for handling work visas for visiting scholars, as I learned upon consulting the Luxembourg embassy in Washington, DC that this has happened many times. We were forced to decide between going ahead with our travel plans and home care arrangements, or delaying leaving until March for a visa that would not be needed by then as the semester ended in May. Rather than force people to find other housing arrangements for January to March, we went ahead and left the USA on tourist visas, hoping to at least be able to catch the first six weeks of the semester, and continue my work from a location outside of the Schengen Area.[16]

I didn't realize it but I was still using tree logic to help me make decisions, for it turned out that while UniLux advertised that classes began in mid-February, they did not begin for the faculty in the graduate college where I was to be a visiting scholar until the last week of March, and they were not classes that met weekly, they were seminars that met biweekly. I was only able to attend one seminar that my host taught before I had to leave Luxembourg. He was not able to warn me sooner that his seminar didn't follow the university's advertised schedule as he was not sure himself by the time I had to make a decision. He did not know when the seminar would begin until after I was already there. On the positive side, in favor of flat, grass-like structures, there is tremendous flexibility, possibly even improvisation, and this may allow the faculty to be able to plan their schedules to fit their own scholarship needs. On the negative side, the students must be very flexible to find ways to attend the seminars when they are offered (or opt not to attend, since they are not graded anyway, at least that was what I understood from the orientation meeting held for students which I attended). For a visiting scholar trying to make plans as to when to arrive and leave, finding out one would not be issued a working visa in December, and finding out in February that seminars wouldn't begin until the end of March, meant I was only able to attend one seminar before I had to leave Luxembourg. Ah, the down side to grass-like spaces!

I was able to obtain a letter of invitation easily and was offered a shared office space in which to work but was not able to establish any kind of working relationship with anyone other than my host, whom I already had a relationship with from attending conferences over the years. I anticipated being able to work with a strong, internationally diverse group of scholars and students; that is what drew me to seeking a semester as a visiting scholar at the University of Luxembourg. However, the youth of the university and its lack of tree-structure made that goal impossible to reach. Flat multiplicities of *n* dimensions that are a signifying and a subjective led to much diminished opportunities to get to know the students and faculty at UniLux and to have any chances to interact with them. For another visiting scholar, this lack of proper processing of work visa applications led to lack of travel to other conferences in Europe once arriving in Luxembourg, when the scholar learned she could not leave without risking losing her traveling visa. When we complain in long-established universities about the bureaucracy and how difficult it is to change anything, we are complaining about tree logic. However, often we do not notice how well things do work, due to tree logic. Structures are not just hindrances; they are developed to be helpful in many ways. It's the inability for them to adjust and adapt easily to changing conditions that makes them feel so cumbersome. Crabgrass is easily adaptive and adjustable, but hard to manage and predict its movement as a result. Consequently, while there may be multiple entryways to grass-like spaces like UniLux, it is also easy to miss the directions altogether, for the entryways are always in motion.

UniLux is young, and as we learned earlier with the history of UTK, it takes time to start a university. At the beginning, it is common to have fits and starts. The time I spent at UniLux reminded me to appreciate how structures at my own university help us all function, and use the space we share efficiently. We complain about the rules and procedures we must go through to have our classes offered where and when we want, in rooms that have the needed technology, etcetera. Yet, the procedures put in place to schedule room assignments help to make sure that when 27,000 students show up for class in the fall, they will be able to find their classrooms and their classmates and professors will be there too. As a result of visiting UniLux, I appreciate more the cohesive learning community for students and faculty in our program that we are able to establish, and the ways that UTK's tree structure help make that happen. What I experienced at UniLux as a lack of learning community, and what I perceived as diffusion caused by its youth and location, make it harder for the students and faculty to find reasons to come to UniLux as well as reasons to stay.

The country of Luxembourg's reason to get into "the higher education business" was to diversify their investments. It was a business decision. Decisions and designs for the university are being made at the national government level, most of which are based on business reasoning rather than educational reasoning. An example of this is the lack of access to libraries in the evening for scholars such as myself. The reasoning may be because they were used to running schools instead of universities, or it could be that it had to do with the cost of making more security keys, and that cost analysis won out over the need for access to university libraries. Another example of the business mindset had to do with the handling of money in the housing office at UniLux. Again, only one key is made per apartment, although I was not able to find out why. It does not matter that two people are living in the apartment and must therefore coordinate with each other to make sure they both can get into their home, between their varied schedules. There were several couples in our building whom had to do this coordination. The university had no trouble taking a 500 EU housing deposit from me the day I arrived, or charging me for health insurance as an international scholar, but they could not find a way to refund me that money when I left. They could accept my bank debit card for deposits to them but they could not use it for returns to me. By national law one must live in the country for three months in order to be allowed to open a bank account in Luxembourg, so scholars there on tourist visas will never be in country long enough to open their own bank account. The university cannot make refunds by cash or check, only by wire transfer, and USA banks do not have the international swift code number they require to make wire transfers from their bank to ours. I felt like I was caught in a "Catch 22" situation. After five months of trying to find a way to be refunded my housing deposit, I was finally able to receive the money by having UniLux give the money they owed me to my host, who then used his own wiring service to refund me. This is a university being run by its country's business rules, not by its own educational rules. The rules for handling money may be normal, common, and proper from a Luxembourg perspective, but they make it very difficult for international scholars to come to Luxembourg and participate in a community of inquiers. I learned that if UniLux wants to change certain policies, they must address the national government to do so. Yes, it is a small country, and these kinds of policies may make a great deal of sense from a business perspective, but the process they have in place makes running a university cumbersome, indeed, from my perspective.

The paradoxes of trying to function at a crabgrass-like university make one appreciate the ways long-developed structures in older universities help things function (when the semester starts and ends is known five years in advance), and make it clear the lines of responsibility (who takes care of visiting scholar's paperwork, how refunds to scholars outside of country are handled). However, these tree-like structures are less likely to be able to adapt to changes and welcome newness (for example, my previous experience on sabbatical at TC, where no office or housing was available for all space is already taken by those who live and work there). My goal in sharing these stories is to help us understand that universities need both: crabgrass to help them be adaptive and to welcome change, and trees to help them withstand severe weather conditions (droughts, storms, such as recessions and cultural censorship) and temporary fashions.

Conclusion

Deleuze and Guattari develop a rich description of rhizomes in their *A Thousand Plateaus*, which they illustrate through various examples. In reading about deeply rooted arboretum or tree models in contrast to more shallow rooted rhizomatic models, I was struck by how higher education institutions can serve as rich examples of the tensions and issues they bring out in their work. For Deleuze and Guattari, the examples they use pull from their intellectual backgrounds in mathematics, biology, and linguistics, for Deleuze is a linguist by background and Guattari is a biologist by background. I am a philosopher of education by background who was able to relate to their nomads and war machine example the most due to my political philosophical work and having grown up as a military brat with a father who was a career officer in the air force. I could see evidence of their discussion of nomads developing the artistry of war while governments develop the machinery of war in the many museums I toured as I traveled in Western Europe. However, it was my sabbatical experience at UniLux and its connections to my experiences at UTK that illustrated for me what Deleuze and Guattari describe most vividly. That extension to their theory is what I sought to explore here.

For any fishing net we develop to help us catch up what we need to survive in/on the Ocean, any epistemological and ontological theories we use to make sense of our infinite universe, there will always be more than we can possibly capture. We have already established that. What this chapter seeks to explore are the tensions and difficulties we will always experience, between weaving strong threads to hold our fishing net together and needing to adjust those threads, and mend them. We have to be careful as the more durable we make our fishing nets, to help us survive and withstand unpredictable difficulties, the less adaptive our nets become. The more adaptive and flexible our fishing nets are, the more vulnerable they are to being damaged, sometimes even destroyed, when storms come. And, one thing is for sure; storms will come. Conditions will change. How to find a balance is something we must continually work on, there is no end to this process, until we become one with the Ocean again. When we are young we complain about the net being too strong and not adaptive enough, when we are older we worry about the dangers of a net that is not strong enough. Seeking to find a balance seems to be the story of our journeys while we are alive, as we re/weave the diverse nets we pass on to our children for them to re/weave as well.[17]

Notes

1. Gilles Deleuze, *Difference and Repetition*, Paul Patton (Trans.) (New York: Columbia University Press, 1994), originally published 1968; Gilles Deleuze and Felix Guattari, *A Thousand Plateaus: Capitalism and Schizophrenia*, Brian Massumi (Foreword and Trans.) (Minneapolis, London: University of Minnesota Press, 1987), originally published 1980. Page numbering will be within the text as it is only in reference to *A Thousand Plateaus*.
2. My host wishes to remain anonymous.
3. The history of the University of Tennessee is found on the university's web site, http://www.utk.edu/aboutut/history/ accessed 6/8-10/15.
4. Lamar Alexander was the 45th governor of the state of Tennessee from 1979–1987. While governor, Alexander worked on the Carnegie Foundation Commission that published its report as *A Nation at Risk*. National Commission on Excellence in Education, *A Nation at Risk* (Washington, DC: U.S. Government Printing Office, 1983).
5. My key source for information on the reform process at UTK comes from *Reforming a College: The University of Tennessee Story*, with Richard Wisniewski as editor and contributing author, along with 11 essays by participating faculty and graduate students who supported the reform efforts. The book was published in 2000, the year I joined the faculty. Wisniewski stepped down as dean in 1996, with "New College" in place. Clinton B. Allison's *Teachers for the South: Pedagogy and Educationists in the University of Tennessee, 1844–1995* is also a source for UTK's New College of Education story. Holmes Group, *Tomorrow's Teachers: A Report of the Holmes Group* (East Lansing, MI: Holmes Group, Inc., 1986).

6. The departments of Health, Leisure, and Safety and Technological and Adult Education left the college although a few faculty from the leaving departments opted to stay in Education. Allison, *Teachers for the South*, p. 228.
7. Allison tells us: "'Units' was a descriptive, working term for the new subdivisions and was to be replaced by a better designation later, but no suggestion for a better name was accepted." Allison, *Teachers for the South*, Notes, #85, p. 286.
8. Joan Paul, "Riding New Waves," in *Reforming a College: The University of Tennessee Story*, pp. 37–52, 47.
9. Allison tells me that among the sports studies students the students in sports psychology were not so happy with CSE either, finding the theory and language problematic and not aligned with their intellectual interests. Allison tells me: "I eventually (and reluctantly) reached the conclusion that we made a mistake in trying to apply a too strict Cultural Studies 'model' on the diverse group of students." Email sent 6/19/2015.
10. Richard Wisniewski, "Afterword," in *Reforming a College: The University of Tennessee Story*, pp. 191–199.
11. *Ibid.*, p. 192.
12. *Ibid.*, p. 199.
13. The history of Luxembourg and the University of Luxembourg was accessed on Wikipedia, https://en.wikipedia.org/wiki/Luxembourg, and https://en.wikipedia.org/wiki/University_of_Luxembourg, 6/15-18/2015.
14. UTK is located on one geographic site, "the hill," including a law college and an agricultural college with a veterinary school. The university system has other regional campuses but these are located in different parts of the state two to seven hours away (Chattanooga, Martin). One could claim that UniLux having differing locations is typical, due to their being an urban campus. However, the population size of the city of Luxembourg is similar to Knoxville, TN and the population size for the entire country is similar to Knox County. This made the spread of the campus between three diversely different sites feel less "urban caused" to me, and more due to its recent opening.
15. My host gave me feedback on the writing of this chapter, which has helped me even more to see the USA assumptions I brought with me to Luxembourg. I thank him much for this assistance. Any mistakes that continue to exist in my description of UniLux are my own, and reveal my own lack of understanding, they are not my host's responsibility. Emailed feedback received 6/18/2015.
16. The Schengen Area comprises 26 European countries that have abolished passport control at their internal borders. It functions like a single country based on the external borders in terms of border control, although the individual countries still maintain a right to control, thus requiring travelers to still carry their passports. Not everyone in the EU is in the Schengen Area, and some that are not in the EU are in the Schengen Area. Please see https://en.wikipedia.org/wiki/Schengen_Area for more information. Accessed 6/16/15.
17. This chapter was presented in two smaller versions at two conferences, titled "Deleuze's and Guattari's Rhizomes: Higher Education as Trees and Grasses." At the Southeastern Philosophy of Education Society Annual Conference, Asheville, NC, 2016, I presented the UT story, and at the American Educational Studies Association Annual Conference, Seattle, WA, 2016, I presented the UniLux story.

· 4 ·

SKY: INDRA'S NET

Introduction

We have considered different, diverse metaphors so far to help us contemplate the concept of infinity as a starting place for relational ontological theories that have developed in various parts of the world. I began with the Ocean as a symbol for infinity, and described ontological and epistemological theories as the warp and weft threads in our fishing nets that we use to help us give meaning to our experiences and "catch up" or "capture" what we need to survive from the infinite Ocean, while we are distinct from the Ocean, until we become one with it again. In Chapter 1, I turned to a description of William James's radical empiricism as we further explored water, in terms of streams, and concepts as being like nets. In Chapter 2, we explored the Land (Earth) as a symbol of infinity and indigenous concepts concerning Nature in a net of sustainability. In Chapter 3, we considered Plants (trees and grass) as symbols of infinity and rhizomatic models of interconnectivity. In this chapter, I turn to the Sky as another example of infinity that has been referenced in various ways throughout time.

Today we live in a time when many of us are urban dwellers. We have built skyscrapers and designed lighting that glows throughout the night to light up our streets and buildings, thus making the stars and the sky less noticeable to us. In fact, human-made lighting makes it more difficult to even see the night sky (light pollution). However, for many, many years in human development the sky, and the night sky in particular with the stars visible above us, served as a continual source of inspiration and amazement, as well as a reminder of our insignificance. There are more stars in the sky then any human being can count. For many people today, the sky still serves this role of inspiration and amazement, although maybe for a fewer percentage of people then when the metaphor of Indra's Net originated.

In *Relational "(e)pistemologies,"* the sixth chapter, W/holistic Relations, focuses on Eastern and Indigenous epistemological theories, in particular Buddhist and Native American descriptions of their ways of knowing.[1] I have dedicated Chapter 2 of *Relational Ontologies* to re/examining Native American descriptions of their relational ontology, and I would like to use this chapter as an opportunity to re/examine Eastern ontologies as rich examples of relationality. In particular, I will focus on Hua-yen Buddhism, a Chinese form of Buddhism that spans during the T'ang period of the late seventh century. As I described in 2003, Buddhism has a tremendous history of over 2,500 years and a great depth and breadth of scholarship applies to it. In fact, the metaphor of Indra's Net that I want to explore in this chapter dates back further than the T'ang period of the late seventh century, for its roots are found in India's Hindu tradition dating back to the fifth century B.C.

I will turn to Francis H. Cook as my key source, for he has devoted many years as a scholar to the translation and close study of the Hua-yen (meaning Flower Ornament) school of Buddhism.[2] I have sought out other scholars to help me and will turn to them when appropriate, but I find that Cook serves as a key source for them as well. When he was searching the topic as a Buddhist Studies graduate student, Cook found that next to nothing had been written yet on this form of Chinese Buddhism, considered by many to be "the high-water mark of Buddhist philosophical effort."[3] His book, *Hua-yen Buddhism: The Jewel Net of Indra*, is the result of a decade of serious, uninterrupted study that began for him as a graduate student in the program Buddhist Studies at the University of Wisconsin. Cook would be the first to point out that Buddhist scholars will spend their entire lives on close studies of particular systems of Buddhist thought; ten years is a very short amount of time compared to a lifetime. However, it is enough for our needs, as nonspecialists of Asian religion and/or philosophical thought. Fortunately, Cook wrote his book with the mixed nature of readers in mind, trying to be as thorough and accurate as his study demanded while also being accessible to nonspecialists such as myself.

Cook tells us his primary source for his book is a treatise called *Hua-yen i-ch'eng chiao I fen-ch'I chang* (in Chinese), which is a treatise composed by Fa-tsang, the third patriarch of the Hua-yen school, at the end of the seventh century.[4] Cook translated this treatise as part of his studies. Cook's Chapter 1, The Jewel Net of Indra, was later published separately in a book edited by Callicott and Ames, *Nature in Asian Traditions and Thought: Essays in Environmental Philosophy*,[5] which is where I first came across his work and used it in my Chapter 7 of *Relational "(e)pistemologies*," Ecological Relations. I am grateful for the chance to trace Cook's work back to his original full text and to explore the Indian roots of Indra's Net as well. I find it a rich metaphor that continues to inform my thinking and challenge me to think outside of the Euro-western epistemological and ontological net in which I was raised.

I begin with a detailed description of Indra's Net, and then follow its roots back to India and Hinduism. Included in this section will be a description of key *dharmas*, or lessons, of Buddhism. I will then move to consider more deeply two key principles from Indra's Net that the Hua-yen school of Buddhism developed, identity and interdependence. Once again, I am claiming that Indra's Net can serve as an excellent example of a relational ontology, and will try to make that case throughout the chapter.

The Metaphor

Francis Cook's work on Hua-yen Buddhism came to my attention because of his development of the concept *cosmic ecology*. In "The Jewel Net of Indra" (both versions), he begins by reminding us that western man has developed a relationship to the natural world which is based on manipulation and domination. We have already come across these ideas in indigenous philosophy (see Chapter 2). In my own work, I refer to "western" as Euro-western to emphasize the roots of these ideas developed in Europe and can be traced back to ancient Greece. In most cases where other scholars use the term "man," I refer to "humans" to use a more inclusive term, but there are times when it really was "man" that should be held responsible. In the case of the natural world, Euro-western *man's* role has been one of manipulation and domination overall. Women, in general, have held a different relationship to nature as they are connected to nature through their reproductive role in societies. Cook presents a view of nature that stresses the interrelatedness of living beings, in contrast to Sir Francis Bacon's view of nature as something to be forced to reveal herself to us, or the Judeo-Christian view of nature as lower in value to human beings and here to serve us, or the view of nature attributed to Aristotle, the ancient Greek philosopher also described as the father of science, that set scientists on a path of analysis, classification, and isolation. Cook uses the term *cosmic ecology* to describe the Hua-yen school of Buddhism, in order to emphasize how all things live in interdependence. The favorite Hua-yen method of exemplifying the manner in which things exist, according to Cook, is with this image:

> Far away in the heavenly abode of the great god Indra, there is a wonderful net which has been hung by some cunning artificer in such a manner that it stretches out infinitely in all directions. In accordance with the extravagant tastes of deities, the artificer has hung a single glittering jewel in the "eye" of the net, and since the net itself is infinite in dimension, the jewels are infinite in number. There hang the jewels, glittering like stars of the first magnitude, a wonderful sight to behold. If we now arbitrarily select one of these jewels for inspection and look closely at it, we will discover that in its polished surface there are reflected *all* the other jewels in the net, infinite in number. Not only that, but each of the jewels reflected in this one jewel is also reflecting all the other jewels, so that there is an infinite reflecting process occurring.[6]

This image of Indra's Net "symbolizes a cosmos in which there is an infinitely repeated interrelationship among all the members of the cosmos. This relationship is said to be one of simultaneous *mutual identity* and *mutual intercausality*."[7] As we explore these key principles in this chapter, let's begin by tracing the history of the metaphor. Rajiv Malhotra, who describes Indra's Net by citing the same description from Cook that I offer, tells us about its roots in Hinduism, in India.[8]

History of Indra's Net

The Hua-yen School

According to Cook, the Hua-yen school of Buddhism developed and flourished during the T'ang dynasty (618–907) in China.[9] Its roots are from India, from the *Avatamsaka Sūtra*. The Chinese translation of *Avatamsaka* is "Flower Ornament." The first three patriarchs of Hua-yen Buddhism (Tu-shun, Chih-yen, and Fa-tsang) were not aware of belonging to a distinct school called "Hua-yen."

It was not until the fourth Patriarch, Ch'eng-kuan (783–839), that a separate school of Buddhism was recognized. The "patriarchs" of Hua-yen just saw themselves as Buddhists especially attracted to one particular scripture, not one that was necessarily more correct, but one that was viewed by them as more complete. They were not "patriarchs" in any strong sense. However, Cook credits the third patriarch, Fa-tsang, with being in fact the real creator of what is now known as Hua-yen.

Hua-yen created no new school of philosophy, what it did instead was bring together different strands of Buddhist thought and form what Cook refers to as "a great syncretism."[10] Hua-yen came to serve as the philosophical base for the other schools of Buddhism. Its key ideas or principles are: no mutual exclusion, and mutual complementarity, both of which we will explore extensively below. Hua-yen is the philosophy of Zen and Zen is the practice of Hua-yen. Hua-yen offers a school of Buddhism to Buddhists who delight in the ordinary, the simple, and the humble. It offers a totalistic view of existence and a particularistic view of existence. The study of Hua-yen Buddhism is never meant to be an end in itself. The goal is to free people from greed, hatred, and ignorance (which is the goal of all Buddhism).

Buddhist Roots in India

Much of the *Avatamsaka Sūtra* (hereafter referred to as the *Sūtra*, which means a story told to make a point) was composed outside of India, Cook tells us, and is more Chinese than Indian as Hua-yen is mainly concerned with causation. However, two very important parts of the *Sūtra* were composed in India and exist in Sanskrit. The "Ten Stages" (*Daśabhūmika)*—is one of the most crucial chapters of the larger *Sūtra*; it inspires the structure of the whole thing. The other chapter that exists as a complete original Sanskrit version is the *Gandavyūha*. It is important to understand that Hua-yen Buddhism incorporates all the *dharma* theory: the doctrine of anātman (no self), the ten stages of a Bodhisattva's career, the doctrines of emptiness and "mind only," the dialectic, Buddha nature, and the womb of Buddhahood. But, Hua-yen teaches something new in Buddhism too, or at least more fully develops two lessons: "the universe as infinitely repeated identity and interdependence of all phenomena."[11] It is safe to say that the Chinese inherited all the concepts of Indian Buddhism.

These key *dharmas*, or lessons, can be traced back to India and are ones I discuss in more depth in *Relational "(e)pistemologies*." However, let me recap some of that discussion of *dharmas* here.[12] I begin this description by pointing out that what I describe as separate lessons are very much intertwined and interconnected. All Buddhists embrace the four Noble Truths: the truth of suffering, the origin of suffering, the cessation of suffering, and the path to the cessation of suffering. The path to the cessation of suffering is the Eightfold Path: right view, right thinking, right speech, right action, right way of life, right endeavor, right mindfulness, and right meditation. The four Noble Truths are often misinterpreted as being fatalistic, due to their focus on suffering, and Buddhism, in general, is perceived as pessimistic and defeatist. However, all sects of Buddhism agree that we must begin by seeing the experience of life as it is: birth, aging, illness, and death, all perceived as suffering. Buddhists consider their realism to be hopeful and joyful for they know how to end suffering. They believe that "the cause of suffering is delusion; eliminating delusion is eliminating suffering; and the way to eliminate delusion is set forth in the Eightfold Righteous Path of conduct."[13] Eliminating suffering leads to exhilaration and liberation.

A fundamental belief of all Buddhists is the dharma of dependent co-origination, or co-arising (*pratïtya samutpäda*), a teaching "that all things exist because of their relations with other things."[14] For Buddhists, the world of phenomena or appearances, and this includes the self, is a relative world empty of inherent existence. Appearances come into being through dependent co-origination, and they are neither existent nor nonexistent. All Buddhists believe that appearances arise from the mind, what Suzuki calls "big mind" or "mind-only" or "essence of mind" or oneness. Our original mind is empty, a ready mind, a nondualistic mind, with no thought of achievement and no thought of self. It is the beginner's mind, the mind of compassion which is boundless.[15]

We are free from extremes when we realize that emptiness and dependent co-origination are one and do not contradict each other. "This thingness of things, as they are, is what is called 'emptiness,' `*sünyata*, the actual isness quality of things."[16] The mind is empty *and* luminous, meaning unobstructed. It is nonthought, nonconcept, the state of unity. David Loy helps us further understand the concept of `*sünyata*: `*Sü* "means 'to swell' in two senses: hollow or empty, and also full, like the womb of a pregnant woman."[17] Our English translation only captures the first sense, empty, and it misses the fullness sense of `*sünyata*: `*Sünyata* means that the true nature of the world is empty/full of all description and predication, and entails the nonexistence of any self-sustaining object "behind" a percept.

Buddhism does not reject all sense-perception, as some falsely accuse it, rather it rejects compound perceptions (*savikalpa*) for "bare" percepts (*nirvikalpa*), which do not provide some knowledge to someone about something.[18] Buddhism recommends that we should return to the initial stage of perception, prior to conceptual influence. "Bare" perception is nondualistic, where there is no seer to see and nothing to see. It is empty/full (*`sünyata*). Nondual perception escapes the main problem of Euro-western theories of perception: how can I even have knowledge of things if those things are separate from my mind? Nondual perception is prior to the bifurcation of mind and matter.

The doctrine of *anātman* (no self, or egolessness) is the surrendering of the ego and the ceasing to believe in the existence of a persistent, continuously existing, single, independent self. Buddhists believe that there is no eternal and unchanging substance in the ego.[19] All phenomena, including the self, come into and go out of being as a consequence of mutual dependence. The term "self" signifies a relation rather than an entity. The *dharmas* of impermanence, emptiness/fullness, and the nonsubstantiality of the self are the way to Enlightenment.

Buddhists believe that Buddha nature (*tathagata-garbha*), which can be defined as simply unconditioned awareness of the nature of mind (big Mind), is inherent in the mind of all beings. This unconditioned awareness is our basic nature and it is always already there. It is primordial, it is prior to and so free from all relative reference points. It is not that all sentient beings *have* Buddha nature, "it is that 'sentient being' refers to everything, and everything *is* the Buddha nature."[20] Buddha nature transcends conceptual mind. Achieving Enlightenment means recognizing one's own mind as unobstructed, perfect emptiness, and fullness, already containing all the Buddha qualities.[21] Buddha nature is inherent in every sentient being and is the most precious of all things.[22]

We find in Indian Buddhist literature that this seed or potential is merely a seed. Training is necessary to mature the seed. Contrary, in Chinese Buddhist literature Buddha nature is not a seed that has to grow; it is already the flower. Beings are already Buddha's, in reality there is nothing to be attained. "The Buddhist faith may be described as a discipline for putting oneself in agreement—establishing life resonance—with the universal Buddha nature."[23]

If we turn to the ontological and epistemological fishing net metaphor I have introduced in this book and use it to help us translate these key Buddhist *dharmas*, we can understand that Buddhism seeks to help us become aware of the conceptual net we use to make sense of our experiences, and how that net can be helpful as well as harmful. It can help us survive, and it can cause us great suffering. The pattern of our lifetimes seems to be this: inheriting the fishing net our families and communities give us, making an effort to re/weave and strengthen that ontological and epistemological net, and then learning how to let go of the net, and the dualisms, misconceptions, and obstructions it can cause us to have. Buddhism draws our attention to all that is spilling out over the top of our fishing nets, and through the holes of our nets, and tries to show us that if we just let go of our nets, we will be free of all the suffering they cause us. It is scary, the idea of "letting go," but it is delusional to think that in the end we can avoid "letting go." Once we realize that we can end suffering if we let go of our fishing net, we can be free of the binds of our nets and stop striving to gather and capture sustenance within our nets. We can experience the exhilaration, liberation, and boundless compassion that come with awakening to our infinity, represented here as the Sky and Indra's Net.

Hinduism's Connection to Hua-yen Buddhism

Rajiv Malhotra tells us

> The metaphor of Indra's Net originates from the *Atharva Veda* (one of the four Vedas), which likens the world to a net woven by the great diety Shakra or Indra. The net is said to be infinite, and to spread in all directions with no beginning or end. At each node of the net is a jewel, so arranged that every jewel reflects all the other jewels. No jewel exists by itself independently of the rest. Everything is related to everything else; nothing is isolated.[24]

Malhotra's work aims to establish the place of Hinduism among the world's traditions and to defend Hinduism from misunderstandings and false myths perpetrated by the Euro-west (and now influencing Indians' own understandings of Hinduism). He tells us that the "notion of an organic unity is a signature of Hinduism, and distinguishes it from all major western religions, philosophies, and cultures."[25] Each individual part is contingent upon, and relative to, the existence of the whole and of all the other parts. The whole and the parts are inseparable. Nothing exists outside of the net. The jewels of Indra's Net are not meant to symbolize static substances. Each jewel is a reflection of other jewels, and individual jewels always remain in flux. Everything in Indra's Net is perpetually in flux. Reality is always in the flux of becoming.

Who is a Hindu? Malhotra's argument is that the "isms" associated with Indian civilization are all Anglicized markers (Hinduism, Buddhism, Jainism, and Sikhism). He describes how the people of India came from the forests, and another "apt metaphor to describe the Hindu worldview is that of a forest" which is diverse and rich with variety.[26] Hinduism did not develop in the desert, where Judeo-Christianity developed. Hindus believe that we are all originally divine, *not* originally sinners. They also believe that each of us is responsible for his or her past karmas, and they reject history centrism, which is built into Judaism, Christianity, and Islam, as we discovered in Chapter 2. Hindus believe in reincarnation, that our pasts are interwoven with all living creatures of all kinds and that our lives are cyclical. We carry the seeds of Enlightenment within us but we must be reborn until we reach Enlightenment, we must grow and blossom.

Malhotra describes Hinduism as diverse and thriving, an ecosystem that continues to adapt and evolve. "In India, a forest suggests fertility, plurality, adaptation, interdependence, and evolution. [...] Hinduism's spiritual outlook rests on this very principle: that the divine is immanent and inseparable from life and nature in all its forms."[27] Hinduism is an "open architecture," with no single founder, no linear history (as such), and no canon on which authorities can agree. There is an absence of a central authority such as the Pope in the Roman Catholic Church. Hinduism accommodates the diversity of faiths. Malhotra suggests that the banyan tree is a good symbol of Hinduism because it "has no well-defined center, because it has multiple roots, trunks, and branches are all interlocked and inseparable. It is, in effect, polycentric."[28]

We have established in this section what the parent ideas of Buddhism are, that the Chinese inherited from India. What we will turn to next is a discussion of what the Chinese did with these parent ideas. Cook's work seeks to establish that while Hua-yen Buddhism incorporates all the doctrines of Buddhism inherited from India, "it also has something special and distinct to offer as a tradition."[29]

Hua-yen Buddhism's Contributions to Buddhism

Cook informs us that "(p)rimarily the doctrine of emptiness is an attack on the conceptual mode of grasping the world."[30] It is his contention that in India, emptiness has mainly an epistemological force, emphasizing a *way of knowing* that relies on intuition and insight. We learn from India, the problem with words and concepts are that they have a purely provisional status, and a purely utilitarian value. We forget that words and concepts are our creations to help us make sense of our world, our experiences, and we begin to believe that the words point to *real* objects that are "out there." We weave nets with our words and concepts, to help us capture up and grasp what is really a continually changing, flowing world (our Ocean, or our Sky). "It is the fundamental teaching of Buddhism that there is only incessant change, or flux, and that there is nothing which undergoes the changes."[31]

While India's Buddhism, with its roots in Hinduism, focuses on a *way of knowing*, the Chinese contribute their Hua-yen Buddhist perspective to Buddhism by helping us consider the doctrine of emptiness in terms of epistemology *and* ontology. They were able to interpret "emptiness" in a positive manner without hypostatizing emptiness, without falling into the error of even greater attachment to the world, without abandoning the basic Buddhist conviction that ordinary experience is delusive and destructive. The main difference between Indian and Chinese Buddhism is that "the Chinese chose to emphasize the point that *emptiness is interdependence*. But interdependence is also emptiness" [...].[32] They describe a net of interconditionality that is infinite in scope. There is *no thing* to change, only change.

As we have already learned, in Indian Buddhist literation, the idea that "all beings are the womb of Buddhahood" is portrayed as potential, or merely a seed. Training is necessary to mature the seed, and this can come in the form of meditation, breathing exercises, and/or yoga, for example. It will likely take multiple reincarnations to achieve Buddhahood. Cook's contention is that by the time of Fa-tsang, the Chinese had grasped the Buddhist concept of *emptiness* correctly, and they were able to be truly creative with it. In the Hua-yen Buddhist use of emptiness in terms of epistemology *and* ontology, the translation becomes: all things *are* Buddha nature, *not* all things *possess* Buddha nature. Hua-yen Buddhism was able to retain a positive, even joyous, appreciation of the absolute value of each facet of this being. Indian literature reduces all things to the common level of insignificance in order to achieve emptiness, whereas Hua-yen Buddhism raises all things to the common level of supreme value.[33] We can see this in the metaphor of Indra's Net, as the net is beautiful; it is full of jewels, an infinite amount of jewels, each of which are beautiful in their own right, and each of which reflect the beauty of all the jewels around them, to infinity. This is not a metaphor that reduces all things to insignificance; it is a metaphor that raises all things up to supreme value.

The two key ideas or principles Hua-yen Buddhism contributes to Buddhism, through the image of Indra's Net, are the concepts of mutual identity and mutual intercausality, and since Cook dedicates a chapter to exploring each of these principles extensively, I will dedicate a section to each one.

Identity

In *Hua-yen Buddhism*, Cook gives us another metaphor to help us understand the concept of mutual identity. It is a metaphor about ten coins that comes from his translation of Fa-tsung's teachings. Before I share that metaphor, though, as well as another one that might help, I'd like to stay with Indra's Net, and see if we can't use it to help us understand this concept of mutual identity. Cook tells us: "the uniqueness of Hua-yen lies in its portrayal of a universe in which the distinct things that constitute it are fundamentally identical and exist only through a complex web of interdependency."[34] Each jewel in Indra's Net is individual, its own jewel, with its own beauty and significance. Maybe one is a ruby, another is a diamond, and another is a pearl.[35] At the same time, all the jewels are identical as well, as they are all jewels in Indra's Net. And, they only exist as part of what makes up Indra's Net; all of them together are what we describe as "Indra's Net."

Cook tells us that it is similar to considering our nose on our face, in that our nose is uniquely a nose, and ours, and yet it is only our nose because it is on our face. I can imagine removing my nose and still having a face, but it would not be the same face. My nose is essential to this face as I know it, without *this* nose, *this* face would be different. However, at the same time my nose is always changing, as it gets dirty, or dry, or wet, or oily, or wrinkled, or sunburned. Maybe I develop freckles on my nose, or a pimple, or skin cancer, as my mother did, and maybe my nose changes temporarily (until the pimple or sunburn goes away), or permanently, as my mother's did when her doctor surgically removed the skin cancer and grafted new skin on her nose which came from her less sun-damaged stomach area. My mother's "new nose" changed the look of her face that I was familiar with, and yet I still knew it was my mother's face. I just had to adjust my image of that face to include her new nose.

It may help to think about the concept of mutual identity at a cellular level, and consider my (your) body as being like a universe to our individual cells. What's nice about this image is it is easier to be reminded that our cells are always in flux, changing, dividing, and dying, and being recreated, born again. We see a solid body, and yet scientists tell us our bodies are mostly made out of water, and that our entire body is remade anew every seven years. That's how long it takes for all our cells to be replaced. Clearly we are in a state of flux. At a cellular level, my cells are individual and unique, in that my cells in my heart are different from the cells in my stomach, bones, or on the surface of my skin, or within my mouth. At the same time, my heart has many cells and they are all heart cells that make up what is described as my heart. Those cells share a mutual identity, as heart cells. And yet, red blood cells are continually flowing in and out of my heart, reminding us that my heart is porous indeed; to be a heart that is living and beating it only exists with those red blood cells as well. And if we step back, all these cells with their unique identities, and their mutual identities, and their interdependent identities only exist because they are inside the universe that is "me."

Another image used in Hua-yen Buddhist teachings by Fa-tsung to symbolize the totality of existence and examine the relationship among them is "the ten coins analogy."[36] Imagine ten coins symbolize the totality of existence, and the relationship between any one coin and the remaining others represents the relationship between anything and infinity. Start with coin 1, and analyze its relationship to the other nine coins singly and collectively. Then we can say coin 1 is identical with coins 2 and 3, all the way to 10. Why? Coin 2 is the result of coin 1; from the standpoint of coin 1, coin 1 is the cause and coin 2 is the result. Coin 1 *exists* (is an independent phenomenal object) and coin 2 is *empty* (exists only in a conditioned manner). The same can be said for coin 3, seen from the perspective of coin 1. The same relationship of cause and effect and the same status of existence and emptiness pertains between coin 1 and each of the remaining coins.

But, Cook tells us, this is still not identity: "(i)dentity can be seen when it is recalled that *no* thing enjoys an independent existence." Everything enjoys a merely conditioned existence and is consequently empty. This is true of coin 1 too; it too is empty for it is coin 1 only in the context of the totality. It is conditioned by coins 10, 9, 8, 7, [...] to coin 2. "The coins are identical in their simultaneous possession of the natures of emptiness and existence." The same situation exists for each of the ten coins simultaneously with respect to the remaining coins.

> (S)ince *each* exerts total casual power with relation to the many, each coin must be simultaneously the cause and the caused, existent and empty. Existence is interdependent existence because this causal efficacy is exerted universally, simultaneously, and reciprocally among all *dharmas*. [...] Because causality is constant and multidirectional among all *dharmas*, [...] any *dharma* is always both existent and empty.[37]

We can notice in this description of the principle of *identity* it has been impossible to avoid the principle of *intercausality*. Just as it is impossible to describe the *dharmas* of Buddhism individually without running into them collectively as they are all connected to each other and influence each other. This is the nature of *dharmas*, the causal flow is multidirectional, which is very similar to John Dewey's idea of *transactions* and what I describe in terms of *relationality*.[38] We are learning that "the uniqueness of Hua-yen lies in its portrayal of a universe in which the distinct things that constitute it are fundamentally identical and exist only through "a complex web of interdependency."[39] Let's turn to looking at Hua-yen Buddhism from the angle of intercausality.

Intercausality

We learned in the previous section on identity that the Hua-yen Buddhist teachings by Fa-tsung recognize the pure facticity of the individual (the jewels in Indra's Net, our unique nose on our individual face). We learned about the individual's dynamic nature, as illustrated in my example of the human body with how the heart has its own individual dynamic nature and is made of individual cells that are uniquely suited to the tasks of the heart and its functions within the circulatory system to keep the human body (the universe in our example) alive. While the heart has its own essence, still, it must work with other systems in the body that have their own natures as well, such as the stomach and the lungs, in order for the body to live and thrive. What this illustrates is a need for supporting conditions by each individual system within the body, or, as Cook describes this, "by each casual *dharma*, which results in a universally pervasive intercausality which is of the nature of interpenetration of *dharma* and *dharma*."[40] Cook uses the term *intercausality*, by which he means "the interpenetration of one thing with another," to make clearer Fa-tsang's concept of *interpenetration*, meaning "a *dharma* considered to be the cause includes within it, by a kind of borrowing or usurpation, the qualities possessed by the contributing conditions."[41]

If we stay with the heart and human body example, the heart borrows, and includes within itself, oxygen from the red blood cells circulating through the heart by way of the circulatory system, and only by absorbing that oxygen, and nutrients from the stomach, for example, is it able to beat, and its beating keeps the circulatory system moving and able to bring the heart more energy and oxygen. The beating of the heart, the breathing of the lungs, the digestion of food, all work together to keep the human body (our example of a universe to the cells inside) alive. As Cook describes this: "Since any *dharma*, seen from the standpoint of itself, possesses the qualities of all the aiding conditions within itself, and since everything in existence is a condition aiding the one *dharma*, then there is an infinite interpenetration of all *dharmas*."[42] In the example of the human body representing the whole universe, infinity, we can understand that the causal flow is multidirectional.

The example Fa-tsang uses in his description of intercausality, or interpenetration, is of a barn, and a rafter in the barn. A rafter can be identified as a rafter on its own, but in order for it to be a rafter, it needs a building so it can fulfill its function. And the building, in this case a barn, can be labeled a barn without needing a particular rafter, but the barn needs these rafters in order for it to be this barn. One way of looking is in terms of the essence of X (identity), and the other way of looking is in terms of the function of X (interpenetration). Identity and interdependence are simply two expressions for the same phenomenon. If there are no distinct parts, such as rafters or nails, there would be no building (which is the error of annihilation). A barn without distinct rafters and nails represents the error of eternalism. If the parts and whole do not become integrated, they are annihilated or eternalized. "*Dharmas* are said to be identical when examined in their static nature and to interpenetrate when examined in their dynamic nature."[43] From a nondualistic perspective, all things have universality and particularity, identity and difference, integration and disintegration.

Conclusion

Buddhists teach us, with the help of many teachers, including Buddha, Fa-tsang, Ikeda, Thich Nah Han, Suzuki, and Francis Cook, that Buddhism is primarily something one does; it is a way of living one's life. It is primarily praxis, not philosophical theory alone; it is an endless task of having right practice, and right attitude, which leads to right understanding. The *dharmas* are there as lessons to help guide us in our practice. Everyone has to find their own way of practicing, of living their everyday lives joyfully and calmly, being very observant, careful, and alert, but doing so without effort. Buddhism is selfless, compassionate action, a striving to ceaselessly benefit others, and in doing so we benefit ourselves. In this way it is: "one hand washing the other." Buddhism encourages us to have attitudes of respect, gratitude, fairness, and compassion, and to use what is necessary for our survival with respect and gratitude, with frugality and fair-mindedness, very similar to what we learned in Chapter 2 from Native Americans. Cook ends his book by bringing us back to Indra's Net this way:

> The interfusion, the sharing of destiny, is as infinite in scope as the reflections in the jewels of Indra's Net. When in a rare moment I manage painfully to rise above a petty individualism by knowing my true nature, I perceive that I dwell in the wondrous net of Indra, and in this incredible network of interdependence, the career of the Bodhisattva must begin. It is not just that "we are all in it" together. We all *are* it, rising or falling as one living body.[44]

This chapter sought to bring to our consideration of a relational ontological and epistemological net, the beautiful example of Indra's Net. We learned how the net is like the stars in the Sky, with the Sky as a symbol of infinity, and the stars as like jewels, representing our mutual identities and interdependence. I have claimed that the ontology and epistemology of Buddhism serves as a powerful example of relationality and have sought to justify that claim through rich examples throughout this chapter. We learned that Buddhism is an example of relationality that shares its roots with Hinduism and comes geographically from the forests of India. It has spread its net over much of the continent of Asia. But, what about Africa? I turn there next, to consider ontological and epistemological nets of interconnectivity that developed there in the form of spider webs.

Notes

1. Barbara J. Thayer-Bacon, *Relational "(e)pistemologies"* (New York: Peter Lang, 2003).
2. Francis H. Cook, *Hua-yen Buddhism: The Jewel Net of Indra* (University Park, PA: The Pennsylvania State University Press, 1977).
3. *Ibid.*, p. x.
4. *Ibid.*, p. xiii. Cook spells out which translation and secondary sources he used to help him on this page. He's using the Japanese edition, numbered 1866, vol. 45, pp. 477–509. *Taishō* edition.
5. Frank Cook, "The Jewel Net of Indra," in *Nature in Asian Traditions and Thought: Essays in Environmental Philosophy*, J. Baird Callicott and Roger T. Ames (Eds.) (Albany, NY: State University of New York Press, 1989): pp. 213–229.
6. Cook, *Hua-yen Buddhism*, p. 2.
7. *Ibid.*, p. 2.
8. Rajiv Malhotra, *Indra's Net: Defending Hinduism's Philosophical Unity* (India: *Harper Collins Publishers*, 2014), ebook. 2015. My notes are from the ebook.
9. See Cook's Chapter 2, The Hua-yen School, pp. 20–33.
10. *Ibid.*, p. 25.
11. Cook, *Hua-yen Buddhism*, p. 35.
12. Thayer-Bacon, *Relational "(e)pistemologies,"* see Chapter 6, pp. 156–168.

13. John Galtung, and Dai-daku Ikeda, *Choose Peace: A Dialogue Between John Galtung and Dai-daku Ikeda*. R. L. Gage (Trans. and Ed.) (London, East Haven, CT: Pluto Press, 1995), Ikeda, pp. 86–87.
14. *Ibid.*, Ikeda, p. 31.
15. Shunryu Suzuki, *Zen Mind, Beginner's Mind*, Trudy Dixon (Ed.) (New York and Tokyo: Weatherhill, 1970), p. 22.
16. Chogyam Trunga, *Glimpses of Abhidharma* (Boulder, CO: Prajñä Press, 1978), p. 37, my italics.
17. David Loy, *Nonduality: A Study in Comparative Philosophy* (New Haven and London: Yale University Press, 1988), p. 51.
18. *Ibid.*, p. 50.
19. Arnold Toynbee and Dai-saku Ikeda, *Choose Life: A Dialogue between Arnold Toynbee and Dai-saku Ikeda*, R. L. Gage (Ed.) (Oxford: Oxford University Press, 1989), p. 335.
20. Paul Williams, *Mahäyäna Buddism: The Doctrinal Foundations* (London and NY: Routledge, 1989), p. 114, emphasis in original.
21. Jamgön Kongtrül, *Cloudless Sky: The Mahamudra Path of the Tibetan Kagyü Buddhist School*, R. Gravel (Trans.) (Boston and London: Shambhala, 1992), p. 80.
22. Ikeda, in Galtung and Ikeda, *Choose Peace*, p. 77.
23. *Ibid.*, p. 75.
24. Malhotra, *Indra's Net*, 322 of 7873.
25. *Ibid.*, 322 of 7873.
26. *Ibid.*, 352 of 7873.
27. *Ibid.*, 384 of 7873.
28. *Ibid.*, 415 of 7873.
29. Cook, *Indra's Net*, p. 35.
30. *Ibid.*, p.42.
31. *Ibid.*, p. 40.
32. *Ibid.*, p. 48, emphasis in original.
33. *Ibid.*, p. 49.
35. *Ibid.*, p. 56.
35. I am not sure if my suggestion that the jewels could be diverse, different kinds of jewels is a correct representation of Indra's Net; it is not described in this way in the different sources I have. No mention of the jewels being different in kind is made.
36. Cook, *Indra's Net*, pp. 64–66, emphasis in original.
37. *Ibid.*, p. 65–66, emphasis in original.
38. John Dewey and Arthur F. Bentley, *Knowing and the Known* (Boston, MA: Beacon Press, 1949, 1960), and Thayer-Bacon, *Relational* "*(e)pistemologies*," Chapter 2, pp. 135–139.
39. Cook, *Indra's Net*, p. 56.
40. *Ibid.*, p. 68.
41. *Ibid.*
42. *Ibid.*
43. *Ibid.*, p. 73.
44. *Ibid.*, p. 122.

· 5 ·

SPIDER WEBS: AFRICAN EXAMPLES

Introduction

We have explored various, diverse metaphors used in different parts of the world to help us make sense of our infinite world, and learn how to survive "in it" until we become one with it again. Symbols of our infinite universe have included the Ocean, the Land, the Wind, and the Sky. We have encountered the infinite with various names as well: God, Buddha, Indra, Great Spirit, and Nature, for example. We have turned to wise scholars from various traditions to help us understand how we weave various weft (ontological) and warp (epistemological) threads to form nets that help us catch our diverse experiences and give them meaning. I have used various examples of "nets" to help us make sense of this process, from fishing nets on our Ocean to Indra's jeweled net in our Sky.

William James's *radical empiricism* helps us understand how our concepts work like a net, trying to capture what is always beyond words, *pure experience*, in Chapter 1. Vine Deloria, Jr., Gergory Cajete, and Winona LaDuke help us understand that indigenous tribal communities have woven richly developed spiritual nets that show us how to live a *sustainable life* with Nature in Chapter 2. Gilles Deleuze and Félix Guattari describe a rhizomatic model that serves as an excellent example of tensions between *rootedness* and *adaptability* in a relational ontology. In Chapter 3, we explore their description of rhizomes in terms of trees and grasses and learn how it could be applies to examples in higher education. Francis Cook helps us understand the Hua-yen school of Buddhism as an example of *cosmic ecology*, as we explore two key principles of *identity* and *interdependence* in Chapter 4.

In this chapter, I want to turn to the continent of Africa for examples of relational ontologies. Scientists theorize that the continents we know today as the Americans, Europe, Asia, Australia, and Africa are what remains from our last supercontinent on our planet Earth, Pangaea, formed by the movement of tectonic plates about 270 million years ago and then separated due to tectonic plate movement about 200 million years ago. The continent of Africa represents the heart of what was Pangaea. Africa, as a continent, is incredibly diverse with approximately 1,000 different languages spoken, and it has the longest recorded history of people living on Earth. Human remains that are approximately 195,000 years old have been found in the Rift Valley of Ethiopian, known as "the rooftop of Africa." It is overwhelming to consider trying to represent the rich diversity of ontological and epistemological nets from Africa in one chapter of a book.

However, it is not necessary to claim that is my task. I only want to develop some key threads, or principles, that traditional African cultures share in common. I cannot claim expertise in understanding these principles, but I don't need to make that claim either, as there are strong African philosophers I can turn to for help. What I have found, in my search for key African philosophers, is that the history of this work is similar to what has happened with Native American philosophy, and feminist philosophy. European missionaries who learned local tribal languages, became spokesmen for the tribal nations and wrote the early writings about various American tribal nations. Similarly, European "outsiders" who lived in Africa, learned the local language, and then served as translators and wrote the early writings about various African tribal nations. Not only did "outsiders" write the information, but they often fell into the trap of over-generalizing their translations beyond that particular tribe. This is the case with Placide Tempels's *Bantu Philosophy*, for example, written in 1945. Tempels was not from the Bantu tribe, he was a Belgian priest who spent many years living in the lower Congo working with the Baluba (plural for Luba).[1]

Similarly, "negritude" and the "negritude movement" was launched in the 1930s in the Latin Quarter of Paris by Leopold Sédar Senghor, a Senegalese statesman, who was educated in Dakar in Senegal and at the Sorbonne in Paris.[2] In alliance with other contacts Senghor made in Paris, and drawing from the Harlem Renaissance in the USA, with influences by African Americans such as Langston Hughes and W.E.B. DuBois, Senghor argued that the African experience of the world is based on emotion, not reason. Feminists know this line of reasoning all too well, for women have historically been described as relying on their emotions and their intuition, not reason, to make sense of their experiences. Radical feminists such as Mary Daly and Paula Gunn Allen, have tried to turn these women's ways of knowing into assets, but it is at too big of a price to pay, for it denies women's abilities to reason, relinquishing that important thinking tool to Euro-western male philosophers.[3] Similarly, negritude claimed the value of emotions for Africans at the price of denying their abilities to reason. This earlier African philosophical work is described by traditional philosophers as ethnophilosophy.[4] My work has been described in a similar way.[5]

Some of the scholars whose work I find helpful in understanding African philosophy and I thought were from Africa have turned out *not* to be from Africa, Richard Bell, for example; or to be from South Africa, but as a white South African, Augustine Shutte, for example. Richard Bell's book, *Understanding African Philosophy*, was sent to me by a scholar in Ethiopia, after my request for help in finding sources. It turns out, Bell is from the South in the USA, where I live and work, and he has spent 25 years working on a cross-cultural understanding of African philosophy, with help in achieving an understanding of African philosophy developed through what he calls "aesthetic consciousness," exposure to African music, dance, stories, etc. He has a connection to Stellenbosch University's philosophy department.[6]

Augustine Shutte, a white South African, who wrote *Philosophy for Africa*, was cited as one of the world's leading scholars on *ubuntu*, a key ontological thread in Africa's spider web, along with Mogobe Ramose, a black South African, who wrote *African Philosophy Through Ubuntu*.[7] Ramose obtained his PhD at the Katholieke Universiteit in Leuven, Belgium and he has worked in Belgium, Zimbabwe, back to Belgium, and then South Africa. Both of these scholars were cited by Samuel Imbo, a Black African professor of philosophy at Hamline University, in Minnesota, USA, who earned his undergraduate degree in Kenya, and his graduate degrees at Purdue University in Indiana, USA. They were also cited by other African scholars such as Dion Foster, who is an ordained minister of the Methodist Church of South African, and a faculty member of theology at Stellenbosch University, as a white South

African.[8] The roots of African philosophical work seem to be more rhizomatic and grass-like, then like deeply rooted trees. However, the key principles I want to explore are traditional and very deeply rooted: *ubuntu*, more accurately expressed as *umuntu ngumuntu ngabantu* (a person is a person through other persons) and *seriti*, "the fundamental energy of the universe" which is neither purely material nor purely spiritual.[9] I must trust that all the scholars whose work I have read will help me fairly describe strands in the spider web of African philosophy.

I have had the good fortune to travel to various African countries on a couple of occasions, Ghana and Ethiopia so far, to work with colleagues from various countries, in particular Sierra Leone and South Africa, and to have several students from different parts of Africa in my classes. Each time I have traveled to Africa, I am reminded of how much I make sense of my experiences through the Euro-western epistemological and ontological fishing net I inherited at my birth and have continued to mend and reweave in my own lifetime. Those travels help me see some warp and weft threads in my net that I was not even aware existed, and they help me notice more of what my net catches to sustain me and what that net lets spill out over the top and through the holes of my ontological and epistemological threads. The direct experiences strongly help me recognize shared principle threads I continue to develop in my rewoven net of relationality. They also serve as a continual reminder of the damage that has been done to Africans' epistemological and ontological nets as they were ripped and torn through Euro-western slavery and colonization. What's important to notice, and honor, is the strength of key threads in African nets, which have survived and continue in their resilience into a postcolonial world. They are a tremendous source of spiritual and intellectual wisdom for us all.

It is fitting to turn to stories from Africa for this chapter as Africa has a rich oral tradition, although it is problematic to focus on oral traditions at the risk of perpetuating a Euro-western myth that Africans did not develop written languages until they were colonized. This myth ignores Africa's rich written histories, for example, in East Africa, that include countries such as Egypt, and its well-known hieroglyphs, but also the Tifinagh alphabet still actively used for writing Berber languages, and the Ge'ez script still used today in Ethiopia and Eritrea. The route I will be taking for this richly diverse continent includes Ghana, South Africa, and Ethiopia, with the stories coming from my own travels as well as from folktales (origination stories) to help set the tone for this chapter.

Ananse, the spider, will be our guide as we weave spider webs, from West Africa (predominantly from the Ashanti tribe in Ghana, but the spider stories come from the people of Togo in West Africa as well). Ananse is the beloved trickster, a folk-hero known all over Africa by various names. Ananse is spelled Anansi as well and I will use both spellings depending of my sources. He is a wise, lovable rogue, similar to Native American's coyote. West African's brought the Ananse stories with them to the USA as slaves, where the spider is also known as Aunt Nancy. I have told stories of Ananse's adventures and the spider's rivalry with the sky god to my own children, the students in my elementary classes, and now my grandchildren, for they are great stories of the weak versus the strong, and how one can use their cunning to triumph over larger foes. Children around the world can relate to them and enjoy them. The stories are moral lessons and illustrate nicely the key principles I want to explore.

Seriti

Spider Ananse Finds Something

The story starts with the God Wulbari complaining because he is positioned too close to Earth and is getting poked and smoked by the people. He decides to rise some in the sky, but people used him for a towel, and to flavor their soup. The God rises higher and higher. He sets up his court (the animals) and Ananse is their captain. Because of his successful tricks on humans, Ananse begins to boast that he could trick all people and even Wulbari. Wulbari sets up a test for Ananse, challenging Ananse to prove he is his equal (due to his boasts). He asks Ananse to bring him something, *but does not tell Ananse what* something *is. Ananse calls on all the birds on Earth, and each give him a feather, from which he makes a handsome robe. He then goes back up to the Sky and he sits on a top branch outside Wulbari's house. None of the animals know who this large, rainbow bird is. They suggest Ananse might know but Wulbari tells them he sent Ananse off to find* something. *Then Wulbari tells the animals what* something *is: the sun, the moon, and the darkness. Ananse overhears what Wulbari says, and so he goes off and finds these. He brings them all back to Wulbari in his bag. First he pulls out of his bag darkness, and all went dark so that no one could see, not even Wulbari. Then he pulls out the moon, and they could see some. Then Ananse pulls out the sun, and this is what caused us to have blindness, for those who looked directly at the sun were blinded. Spider Ananse has the sense to get* something *for Wulbari. He proves he is equal to God.*[10]

Seriti, the fundamental energy of the universe, is the African word for Being, spirit, life-force. Shutte tells us *seriti* supplies the metaphysical foundation and framework for the conception of persons and communities which we will discuss more in the next section. "It is the notion most fundamental in traditional African worldviews."[11] Tempels describes it like this: "force is the nature of being, force is being, being is force." "The human being is like a live electric wire," *seriti* is "like an aura around the human being." "*Seriti* is the energy or power that both makes us ourselves and unites us in personal interaction with others."[12] Shutte describes *seriti* as being broadly metaphysical, and that it applies to an understanding of human nature and community, but it also has an ethical dimension as goodness increases the power of this force, individually and socially. *Seriti* is the key idea:

> that reality is force and the world a process of interplay between forces, that humanity is part of this universal field of force, that at bottom all force is alive, spiritual rather than material, that the individual's life and fulfillment are only to be found in community with others (a community that does not end at death), that morality is the development of natural tendencies to fuller being and more abundant life, and finally that all human life and world process is directed and empowered by a transcendent origin of life and force.[13]

In the Ananse story I shared, Wulbari, God, is in close contact with human beings, he is not separated from humanity. In fact, they are poking him with their walking sticks, he is in such close proximity to them, so he moves a little higher in the sky, but they still cause him discomfort, using him as a towel and to flavor their soup. Animals are not separate from Wulbari either, within daily contact and consultation, so that even as he seeks to move further away from people, because of the discomfort they cause him; he is still in close contact with animals. Ananse can converse with Wulbari, even challenge him, in an effort to prove he is equal to Wulbari. Not only does Ananse make this challenge, but also he succeeds in meeting the challenge and proving he is Wulbari's equal. What an interesting idea, that an animal/insect as small as a spider would be equal to God! Such an idea likely would be considered blasphemy in Christian and Moslem religions; however, it is presented as a humorous story for the Ashanti tribe in Ghana, a loose federation that has existed for over 400 years.

Story Two

My youngest son, Sam, husband/partner, Charles, and I traveled to Ghana in early summer, during the rainy season, the summer Sam turned 12, in order for me to have the chance to observe in a West African school system, as I sought to trace African American cultural expressions in schools back to their cultural roots. Our host in Ghana was the assistant director of Ghana's National Theater, Bernard Woma, and he was going to pick us up at the airport in Accra and take us to his home, to his compound. A compound usually has a wall around the land where homes, kitchens, animals, equipment, and in Woma's case dorms for students to stay, as well as practice and performance areas are located. We were going to pay Bernard to stay there and Sam and Charles were going to take djembe drum lessons from a West African drummer while I was observing in the local school during the day.

Bernard Woma runs a West African dance and percussion school and on his website he described his home as being in "the suburbs of Accra," which turned out to be a small village, Media, two hours away. Bernard and I made all our arrangements via the internet, with him responding within 24 hours each time I emailed him. This gave me the impression he had email access in his home or nearby, when in reality he had access to email by going to an Internet Café in Accra each day when he was in the city for his work, again, two hours away via a very crowded, pot-holed two lane highway that becomes four lanes if the shoulders are used too when traffic is heavy.

When I purchased our plane tickets, the travel agency neglected to tell us we needed visas to travel to Ghana. We fell between the cracks at the travel agency as one agent started on our ticket arrangements then left on maternity leave, and another agent took over her accounts, thinking the first agent had ordered our visas. We showed up at the airport with our tickets, passports, and luggage on the day we were supposed to fly out, only to be turned away as we didn't have the necessary visas to travel to Ghana. This meant rebooking and getting expedited visas, so that we could fly out and I could still see the schools while they were in session. Our original arrangements with Bernard had to be cancelled, and I sent him our new patchwork travel plans and the date and time we hoped to arrive, via email, with much apologies for the changed plans. Two days of missing planes due to thunderstorms and more hobbling together of flights as stand-by passengers, and more emails sent as plans kept changing, and more apologies, then we finally arrived in Accra, Ghana, just as the sun was setting. No one was there to meet us. Later we found out Bernard never received those email messages and had been there to pick us up at the original date and time.

No problem, we hailed a taxi, with a driver who claimed he knew where Media was. Surprise! Two hours later, in the pitch dark, we arrive to Media, where there is one paved road through the middle of the village, and one paved road to an ashram on the edge of the village, and no streetlights. We had an address but could not find any street signs or numbers on the compounds. We could hear drumming, but were not sure to whom it belonged, so, defeated and exhausted we asked the taxi driver to take us back to the airport where there was a hotel, and come back in the morning daylight hours to try again. He agreed, as his fares with us quickly were adding up to a full month's income.

In the sun, next morning, we found Bernard's compound, and we could see that it was within easy walking distance from the ashram. We had been very close to it the night before. Once we were there, we realized, we arrived to Ghana with USA expectations of street signs and address numbers on walls or mailboxes that we would be able to see, when all we had to do was roll down the cab's windows and follow the sound of the drumming. Bernard has the biggest compound in the village, by far, to accommodate his West African percussion and dance school, and for goodness sake, it was drumming *we could hear! The village of Media was full of the vibrant force of music, singing, and dancing, and we totally missed it. We came in with our USA expectations, without realizing we were doing so.*

We did get better, as the week went on, and we realized our foolishness. Charles and Sam took drumming lessons throughout the week I spent in school, and Sam came home with a djembe as his birthday present, the one he used for lessons. And, while we missed that first night's celebration, we did get to participate in another one, and join in with the dancers for hours of singing and dancing with the drums and xylophones playing. In fact, Charles and Sam had a chance to play along.

I tell this story to illustrate how the fundamental energy of the universe was expressed in Media, Ghana, through the music and dance. Ramose describes the African philosophical conception on the universe as musical and dynamic. It does not split reason and emotions. It is an invitation to dance that is not declinable; it is an epistemological and ontological imperative. He talks about the drum, and not being a *passive spectator*. Truth is simultaneously participatory and interactive.[14] The spirit of Being, *seriti*, life force, was vividly expressed that evening. We didn't catch it in our spider web, as we were not paying close enough attention, and had not adjusted yet to the new location in which we found ourselves. We still were trying to use our old net, which is useful where we live, but not where we were traveling. Not only was it not useful, it was costly in how it was causing us near-misses.

I am proud to be able to say I have hosted those dancers and percussionists in my own home in the United States, and I had the chance to pay back their generosity and kindness given to us. I even had the chance to introduce them to basketball and attempt to explain that game to them, a fun gift exchange for the times I watched world soccer matches during my stay with much of the village of Media in attendance at Bernard's house, where the best television and electrical source existed. They never said, "what fools!" to us, they sympathized with our lost time and expense. Then as they got to know us better, they helped us better understand how the mishaps occurred, such as not receiving any email and not having access to any email in their home, where they were conducting a week-long dance and drumming workshop. No one was driving to Accra that week so no one went to an Internet Café. That's when we also learned the effort they had made to accommodate our travel plans, and we laughed about the Euro-western perspectives of common African means of expression. This seems to me a vivid example of how Euro-westerners arrive in Africa with their western nets, and how so much can fall through or be assigned the wrong meaning. It is as though Ananse is playing tricks on us, and the sooner we figure out we need a new net, a spider web instead of a fishing net maybe, the better.

In several of the books I have read about African philosophy, the authors begin by trying to defend that Africans have important contributions to make to philosophy.[15] They describe the kinds of questions philosophers ask, the ways they approach their arguments, and the tools they use to help them justify their claims, based on a Euro-western definition of philosophy. Euro-western philosophy is treated like it is neutral and universal if framed that way and it is allowed to establish the norms for what counts as "good philosophy." In contrast, African philosophy is described as "other," for example, as "ethnophilosophy," that does not measure up to Euro-western standards.[16] It is described as more like literature, or as descriptive anthropology, without awareness that these critiques are based on acceptance of European definitions of philosophy. The descriptions also reflect European definitions of Africa. Definitions of philosophy from European perspectives deny Africa's philosophy, and when the work meets their definition of philosophy there is a denial that the standard-bearing judgment itself is a form of colonization and marginalization. As Imbo points out, a definition of philosophy from a European perspective has far-reaching hegemonic implications.[17]

Care must be made, in claiming philosophical perspectives unique to Africa as well, as these can be romanticized or presented as incommensurable, a similar problem that radical feminist scholars have faced.[18] This is the problem Tempels faced with his presentation of the Bantu worldview. Senghor's negritude theory can be viewed in a positive light for his efforts to define African philosophy for its uniqueness, but then we are back to the problem of incommensurability, as well as the critique that Senghor accepts the European definitions of Africa in his theory. Using European standards to measure African uniqueness avoids questioning the legitimacy of the colonial situation in which the uniqueness arises.

African philosophical literature has been criticized by other African philosophers for being too oriented toward a non-African audience, for dangerously looking backward, and verging on an absolute linguistic relativism, where traditional African thought is presented "as promoting a kind of group mind, an unanimity in social and political life."[19] These are all problems First Nations scholars have faced, and feminist and Black scholars have had to address as well.[20]

Imbo uses Kwame Anthony Appiah's *In My Father's House* as an example of how contemporary African philosophers can avoid the pitfalls of both ethnophilosophy and universalism.[21] The trick is to avoid furthering the status quo of Euro-western philosophy and help contemporary African philosophy come to terms with its history. It is a violent history, with much harm done, for modernity, which comes out of Europe, has led to the destruction of contacted traditional cultures, similar to what First Nations have experienced in the Americas. I am in solidarity with African philosophers' efforts to navigate between their historical situatedness and the project of decentering modernity in ways that allow for a plurality of methods of knowledge production. Like other feminist scholars, I have critiqued Euro-western philosophy's ahistoricism and universalism, its "God trick," as Donna Haraway refers to it.[22] As Ananse's story and my story about arriving in Ghana remind us, we have to be careful not to dismiss experiences and views that do not fit our scheme of the world, as interpreters who may be using nets that are inappropriate for the experiences we are having. We have to be careful not to assume Euro-western philosophy's net is able to capture all in its net, or that it is neutral and inevitable and should not be critiqued by contesting views. Ananse is willing to contest even the views of the gods.

How Anansi Won the Stories of the Sky God

Anansi sat under a tree, bored, wishing he could own one of the stories by the Sky god, because the Sky God kept all the stories locked away (no books, films, television, songs, or dreams). He wondered what it would feel like to own the stories and realized everyone would be jealous. He decided he would try to buy the stories from the Sky God, and so he packed up some food and traveled to the home of the Sky god to ask what they cost. The Sky God smiled and told Anansi many have tried to buy them but no one has succeeded because the price is great. He wants: the Hornets, Python, one of the fairies, and Leopard. "If you can bring me these I'll give you all the stories told so far and all the stories yet to be told." So, Anansi sets out to catch all that the Sky God asks for, and with the help of his wife, they make plans that trick all four beings. When he is able to give to the Sky God the items he asked for, the Sky God is amazed. He is given the pot full of stories and the stories are to be called Anansesem, spider stories, from this day forward, in honor of his great deed. As Anansi ran home to show his wife the pot of stories, he didn't look where he was going and tripped over a root. The lid of the pot came off and the wind caught the stories as they fell and scattered them to the four corners of the World. Anansi's misfortune is our good fortune for the stories belong to all of us now.[23]

Ubuntu

South Africa, or the Republic of South Africa, as it is formally known, is the southernmost country in Africa and the Eastern Hemisphere, bordered by the Atlantic and Indian Oceans. It is also one of the 25 largest countries in the world, with close to 53 million people. It is a multiethnic society with 11 languages officially recognized in its constitution, including Afrikaans (developed from Dutch, as part of its history of colonization), English (due to English colonization), and nine different Bantu languages. South Africa is a country, like Ethiopia, where some of the oldest human remains have been found, dating back at least 170,000 years, in the area known as the Cradle of Humankind. The Xhosa and Zulu Bantu-speaking peoples were living in this land for over 1,000 years when the Portuguese, Dutch, and then the British sought to establish colonies there as part of the East India spice trade. The sea route to India was around the coast of South Africa (the Cape of Good Hope), and Cape Town was established as a place of replenishment for the long journey by sea from Europe to India and back again. The history of the colonial periods of South Africa includes wars between the Zulus and various colonizers, and increased immigration to South Africa due to the discovery of diamonds (1867) and gold (1884). This time period is when we see the beginnings of racial segregation, first by the Dutch, and then by the English, although the control of settlement and movement was mainly informal during the 1800s. By the early 1900s, after South Africa gained independence from Britain in 1910, those in power began restricting native land use and movement more formally, starting with the Natives' Land Act of 1913, that left natives with only seven percent of the country.

By the time I was in high school learning about South Africa's legally institutionalized racial segregation system, known as *apartheid*, it had been in existence for over 20 years, since 1948, and remained in existence in some form or another for 20-plus more years beyond my graduation, until the 1990s. South Africa held its first universal elections in 1994, and Nelson Mandela became the first Black African President of the Republic of South Africa, the very same man who had spent 27 years in prison for the charge of sabotage. 1994 is the same year that Augustine Shutte's *Philosophy for Africa* had a second printing, only a year after it first came out.[24] Shutte explains to us, as a white South African, that while his philosophical training was European, his experience is South African. He worried at the time of his writing that the deepest values of Africa were at stake, due to colonization and the struggle with apartheid. There was a whole generation of South Africans who grew up during the years of apartheid, without learning their families' traditional values, and without hope. What we know now, more than 20 years later, again, is that those deepest values are still alive and well as they were used by President Mandela, and others, to guide South Africa out of apartheid, through more than a year of Truth and Reconciliation Hearings, and on to forgiveness and reconciliation. Black South Africans, overall, did not seek retribution for all the harm done to them; they sought reconciliatory justice. The Truth and Reconciliation Hearings were an effort to restore a balance, not to punish but to restore the dignity of the people. The goal with the hearings, which were broadcast on the television and radio for all to bear witness, was to turn moral indifference, denial, quilt, and shame into personal and social responsibility. Black South Africans' abilities to forgive, which seems limitless and is so inspiring, was guided by the principle of *ubuntu*. Let me tell an Anansi story to help us understand *ubuntu*.

Anansi the Spider: A Tale from the Ashanti

This is the story of Anansi and his six sons: See Trouble, Road Builder, River Drinker, Game Skinner, Stone Thrower, and Cushion. Anansi goes on a long journey and gets lost, and falls into trouble; he is swallowed by a fish. The first son sees the trouble and lets all of Anansi's sons know he is in trouble. The second son builds a road so the sons can get there to rescue their father. The first son sees where Anansi is, inside the fish, and the third son, River Drinker, drinks the river water. The fourth son, Game Skinner, splits open the fish and pulls out Anansi, alive, from inside the fish. But, a falcon flies down and grabs Anansi just then, so the fifth son, Stone Thrower, throws a stone and hits the falcon and Anansi falls from the sky and safely lands on top of the sixth son, Cushion. They go home a happy family. That night Anansi finds a great globe of light in the forest and wants to give it to the son who rescued him, but to whom should he give it? He asks for help from The God of All Things (Nyame), but they cannot decide, so Nyame places it up high in the sky for all to see. The moon is still there for all of us to enjoy.[25]

The story of Anansi and his six sons nicely illustrates the principle of *ubuntu*. Anansi represents one generation in the spider family and his sons represent another. They are the future and Anansi is the present. His sons work together to save him from trouble, and in doing this, harmony is restored to the family/community. The gift Anansi wants to bestow in gratitude for his sons' rescue efforts becomes a gift for all of us.

Dion Forster, a White South African minister who has written about *ubuntu*, cites Mogobe Ramose and Augustine Shutte as the world's leading scholars on *ubuntu*. They are key sources to him, and other South African philosophers and theologians, and I turn to them as my key sources as well. The Southern African philosophy, *ubuntu*, more accurately expressed as *umuntu ngumuntu ngabantu* (a person is a person through other persons) means "humanity, humanness, humaneness."[26]

Shutte tells us that "*umuntu ngumuntu ngabantu*" is a Xhosa expression that is common in all African languages and traditions. Persons are defined by the relationships between them and others. In contrast to Descartes claim, "I think therefore I am," the principle of *ubuntu* claims "I participate, therefore I am." The key idea is: "Self and world are united and intermingle in a web of reciprocal relations."[27] According to Shutte, emphasis on community is African thought's most central and all-pervasive character. It is universally embodied and embedded in customs and institutions, as we can see in the example of South Africa's restorative approach to justice, and we can find in another story I share from my visit to Ghana.

Story Five

When my family and I finally found Bernard Woma's compound, we discovered he was not there. He took the workshop students back to Accra that day to give them a little tour before they caught their flights home. The drums we heard the night before were a goodbye, send off to them. There were plenty of people in the main house when we arrived, including Fortune, the housekeeper and one in charge of cooking/ cleaning, general compound care while students were in attendance. She was everyone's favorite big sister/mother, and we grew to love her too, as she embraced us immediately and welcomed us into the Woma household. As I went around introducing myself to the family members, I asked for names and ages of the children, and whether or not they were Bernard's children (I had never met Bernard, just corresponded with him by email). They all told me he was their father. As the week went on, the children began calling me Auntie Barb. I went to school with them in the mornings and played with them in the evenings. Some even called me Mommie Barb, as I was Mom to Sam, and they saw me mothering him. By the end of my time there, I learned that none *of the children in the home were Bernard's biological children, they were his nieces and nephews. However, as Fortune explained, when a child is born to you, your brothers and sisters are also considered the child's parent, and often your children will go live with them, to help the parent when they need help due to things like illness, loss of jobs, or job possibilities elsewhere, or just because you want your child to experience living in another part of the country where you grew up and your sister still lives. That is where Bernard's biological son and only child was at the time of our visit: with Bernard's sister (his Aunt) experiencing where his father grew up, not living with his father at all while I was there. And, Bernard had his brother's children at his compound as he had the means to care for them that his brother lacked. The brother lived in the same village of Media. The Woma family are a living example of the proverb: "It takes a village to raise a child." I also learned from Fortune that when a parent dies, their wealth is passed on to their nieces and nephews before any is passed on to their own biological children. Even for the president of the country, this was the law when I was there. One can see how this practice of sharing wealth throughout the family protects the entire family's children from unanticipated disasters, and assures everyone's well-being. It is also a good illustration of ubuntu: a person is a person through other persons.*

The children were not lying to me, or trying to confuse me, they did not understand my question the way I did. Once again, I was using my Euro-western epistemological and ontological fishing net to help me make sense of their world, and did not understand the spider web of relationality they use. As Foster describes this: "To be truly human means being in relationship with other persons who give form and substance to one's true humanity."[28] I asked the question, whose child are you? In their spider web of relationality, the answer to who one is, is always in relation to one's ancestors, grandparents, parents, and wider social grouping. Relationships are an active lived reality, and one's true identity does not come from one encounter ("relating") but from a continuum of shared being ("having a relationship"). Persons are fundamentally shaped by being in relationship (not just having a relationship).[29] From this story we also learn that *ubuntu* is *not* a collection of individuals, as collectivism can mean in other parts of the world.

Ramose describes *ubuntu* as the root of African philosophy: "the wellspring flowing with African ontology and epistemology."[30] *Ubuntu* is two words: *ubu* and *ntu*. The prefix, *ubu* = be-ing in general, enfolded be-ing, is always oriented toward unfoldment. The stem, *-ntu* = "the nodal point at which be-ing assumes concrete form or a mode of being in the process of continual unfoldment may be said to be the distinctly epistemological." Ramose explains how *ubuntu* is always a -ness and not an -ism. It is a gerund and a gerundive: be-ing becoming, the incessant flow of motion (not fragmented). The doer do-ing. Always continuous. "The logic of *ubu-ntu* is [...] the logic of and for the preservation of be-ing as a whole-ness."[31] Here we come back to *seriti*, the life force described previously, the universe as always continuous and dynamic.

Ramose recognizes there is tremendous diversity in African cultures, but argues that there is to some extent an underlying unity (similarities).[32] He explains the ontology of *ubuntu* philosophy as having three interrelated dimensions: the living (*umuntu*), those who have passed away, the living-dead (*abaphansi*), and the yet-to-be-born (the future). It's an onto-triadic structure of be-ing (past, present, and future). Ramose explains that human life does not terminate at the death of an individual for Africans. The living-dead are important to the upkeep and protection of the family and community; therefore, it is important that leaders, elders, must have good relations with their living-dead. Africans start from a point of wholeness; how they define personhood, individuals are inextricably linked to the all-encompassing universe. Personhood is acquired, not merely established by virtue of the fact of being human.

For Africans, according to Ramose, the community plays a crucial role in the individual's acquisition of full personhood.[33] Personhood depends on community, upon human relations. The child is born, and needs to establish a covenant with the living-dead (the ancestors). Circumcision is viewed as the initiation to personhood (giving blood to the living-dead). Until the child goes through the operation he is still an outsider. "Once he has shed his blood, he joins the stream of his people."[34] The rite of initiation fulfills three functions: incorporates the person into the living community, links the initiated to the living-dead, and qualifies the child to participate in marriage (the future community, those yet-to-be-born). To be a subject is to be transcendence. It is what Ramose refers to as "metaphysics of presence" and this is the basis for immortality in African traditional thought. Ancestors live as long as their memory lives on (four to five generations). Then they become the nameless dead.

Shutte's worries that the deepest values of Africa were harmed by colonization and the struggle with apartheid seem to be largely unfounded, although in no way do I wish to diminish recognition of the harm done to Black South Africans. However, the deepest values were shown to be alive and well and their strength demonstrated in the Truth and Reconciliation Hearings. The country needed to bare witness to the harm done in order for them to be able to move forward together. The people who suffered from apartheid were not just the present generation, the living community, but also their living-dead (the ancestors), and beyond them, the nameless dead. According to *ubuntu* understanding of the cosmic, harmony must be preserved and maintained, and the way we do this is through reaching consensus. "Peace through the concrete realization of justice is the fundamental law of *ubuntu* philosophy."[35]

Now we can better understand the Truth and Reconciliation Hearings. They were based on the principle of *ubuntu*. It was important that the harms be admitted to and voiced out-loud, that attention be given to the decades of harm done. Amnesty was offered to people for full disclosure of harms done to others. The truth of the past had to be unveiled, not to seek revenge, but in order to find harmony again and restore dignity to those harmed. Richard Bell tells us 21,000 statements were made by victims, and the people of South Africa *all* listened to the cries of the victims.[36] This "living theatre," as he calls it, is a justice of recognition and reconciliation, helping the country and its people find harmony again, through love, forgiveness, generosity, and compassion. Some complained that real social justice was not served, that communities were shattered and livelihoods destroyed by apartheid, and there was no punishment due to the amnesty provision. However, amnesty was not granted to everyone, and those denied amnesty could face criminal prosecution. What prevailed was compassion-based justice. *Motho ke motho ka batho* = to be human is to affirm one's humanness by recognizing the same in others.[37]

The Rooftop of Africa

Ethiopia is located in East Africa, in what is referred to as "the horn of Africa." It is officially known as the Federal Democratic Republic of Ethiopia and its current constitution as a federal democratic republic was accepted in 1995. It is the most populated land-locked country in the world, with over 100 million people, although it has only been land-locked since 2000, when its civil war with Eritrea ended with Eritrea becoming its own country, taking from Ethiopia its border with the Gulf of Aden. Ethiopia now depends on Djibouti for its access to a seaport. Somalia is Ethiopia's neighbor south of Djibouti that could be another possible port, however Somalia teeters on being a failed state as it struggles for stability.

Ethiopia is known as "the Rooftop of Africa," because of its highlands, which cover most of the country. The country's overall landmass is over one million square kilometers (435,071 sq. miles) in size, and the highlands cover most of the area, with an elevation between 2,000 and 2,500 meters (6,562–8,202 feet) above sea level. All of Ethiopia's major cities are in the highlands, including its capital, Addis Ababa. Because of Ethiopia's altitude, much of the country's climate is very pleasant and mild for a country located so close to the equator, between latitudes three and 15 degrees North. The overall temperature range is a comfortable 40 to 70 degrees Fahrenheit, ten to 20 degrees Celsius. It is also sunny most of the time. Ethiopians say that they have too much sunlight, for it makes them vulnerable to droughts. Even in the rainiest season, which is June to September, there is still an average of seven hours of sunlight. The water from Ethiopia's lakes and rivers in the highlands are the source for the Nile River as well as 11 other major rivers, vital to East Africa, even though Ethiopia experiences frequent droughts, some of them severe enough to cause famines. In the 1980s, Ethiopia experienced an extreme drought that caused a famine where 400,000 people died from starvation, although the civil war that Ethiopia experienced during that decade is also to blame for many people dying. Ironically, Ethiopia has the largest water reserves in Africa. There are efforts to help Ethiopia with irrigation and reforestation to help the country manage their food supply through droughts. The country uses hydropower for its electrical source, which means that when it experiences a drought, as it is currently, this affects its electrical power. While I was there the hall lights were off in the University of Addis Ababa in the afternoons to save electricity.

Ethiopia has the Rift Valley running diagonally through it from the south west corner to the north east, and in the Rift Valley the oldest human bones have been found, which explains why Ethiopia is referred to as the original home of humankind. The Rift Valley is famous for its striking geographic features and beauty, and also for its archeological digs. It is there that Australopithecine Lucy (AL 288–1) was found in 1974, and she can be viewed in Ethiopia's National Museum in Addis Ababa. Humans appear to have spread out to the Middle East, Asia, and Europe from the Addis Ababa area over 100,000 years ago.

Ethiopians have great pride in their long, extensive history, which includes: monarchies that can be traced back to the second millennium BC, their written and oral language that is one of the oldest in the world, and their standing in more recent history is that they are the only African country that was never colonized by a European nation. Their military, which is considered the strongest in Africa, was able to hold off colonizing efforts in the 1800s, so that it remained a sovereign nation, although it was occupied by Italy during World War II. Ethiopia became the first African nation to join the League of Nations and later the United Nations. Today it is the host to the African Union.

In the 1970s, when the world experienced an oil embargo that impacted nations at a global level, Ethiopia felt that impact as well. Students and professors protested the high prices of gas, and the cab drivers went on strike. Their last monarch Haile Selassie's reign came to an end in 1974 on his 80th birthday, when he was arrested by the military and a junta occurred, overthrowing the monarchy. Selassie's palace and the grounds surrounding it now form the attractive campus of the Addis Ababa University. The military junta, known as the Derg, became a socialist government backed by the Soviet Union, East Germany, North Korea, and Cuba. During the period that they were in power, which lasted until the USSR collapsed in 1991, 50,000–100,000 people are estimated to have died, pushing the total people dying under the Derg to around 500,000, with the famine and civil war included, although I have read estimates that are even higher. The socialist government executed and imprisoned many of its citizens, fearing another uprising. Those most targeted were the professors and students in the university, those most likely to critique the current government. Ethiopia lost a generation of their best scholars to the Derg.

There is a museum in Addis Ababa that marks this time in Ethiopia's history, called the "Red Terror" Martyrs' Memorial Museum, which I visited while in Addis Ababa. There one can see pictures of many of the victims, and showcases full of their skulls and bones, from the mass graves where they were buried. Another showcase is full of the clothing people were wearing when they were executed, as well as belongings they had on them such as watches and wallets. On the walls are listed names after names of people who were executed, including family members of my hosts.

I traveled to Ethiopia to serve as an external examiner for a doctoral candidate at the invitation of faculty at Addis Ababa University, for it is required by law that someone external to the country must serve as an examiner for the student, to help insure quality of scholarship.[38] That is when I learned so much about Ethiopia, as I visited its museums, read its history, and talked to its people. The country is poor, considered one of the poorest in the world, but it is also one of the fastest growing economies in the world. There is construction work going on everywhere one looks in Addis Ababa, and their economy is getting stronger. They have not had help in building their infrastructure, such as transportation systems, due to never having been colonized, and they are proud of what they have been able to accomplish on their own. However, in the student's defense, I was asked by a scholar in attendance: "Why does the world hate us?" I think the question is in reference to the number of people who have died, during my adult lifetime. I had no answer and the question still troubles me.

Ramose explains in *African Philosophy Through Ubuntu*, that there are concerns for *ubuntu* as a basic principle for law, and for politics.[39] *Ubuntu* is the basis for African law that stretches from the Nubian Desert to the Cape of Good Hope, and from Senegal to Zanzibar. He explains to us that the African view is that law is a lived experience. It is dynamic, attunement to be-ing, based on the other principle we learned, *seriti*. Law (*molao*) is not something prescribed for us to follow; it arises from the concrete experience at a particular time and place, similar to feminist care theory in contrast to principled approaches to law and ethics.[40] *Molao* can never be a substitute for the continuing unfolding of experience.

As we learned with the example of South Africa, there are no limits to the law in terms of a statue of limitations, for the goal is restoration and that is regardless of time when the harm occurred. Traditional African law has a transcendent dimension that is the appeal to the living-dead. The living-dead give their approval. The political is always an ongoing dialogue with the ontological. Ramose tells us the sovereignty of the king, for example, Haile Selassie, derives from and belongs to the people. The king is king by the grace of the people and not by the grace of God. Thus, when it was perceived that the king was no longer taking care of his subjects, it was the right of the people to remove the king.

As we learned in the second section, *Umuntu ngumuntu ngabantu (Motho ke motho ke batho)* means "to be human is to affirm one's humanness by recognizing the same in others."[41] This leads to a relational context, and the principles of human equality, reciprocity, and solidarity. It is a belief in the importance for sharing and caring for one another, as we learned in Bernard Woma's home in Ghana. From an Ethiopian perspective, how could the world stand by and let a half-million people die? Where are the world's caring and sharing and the affirmation of the humanness of the Ethiopian people? I do not know how to answer that question, accept to recognize that the Euro-western fishing net that is strung with threads of individualism, freedom, choice, autonomy, and capitalism, catches up ideas such as "meritocracy" (people get what they deserve based on how hard they are willing to work) and "unlimited resources" (if we all work hard enough we can achieve our dreams of material wealth). It is not an epistemological and ontological net that catches up principles of human equality, reciprocity, and solidarity. It is a net that catches up values of competition, and everyone for themselves; it lets fall through the holes and spill over the top of the net, ideas of relationality, collaboration, and interconnectivity.

Ramose tells us that adversarial politics is foreign to African traditional political culture. The political party in Africa has come to be seen as an instrument of power and domination, as we know happened in South Africa, and we now know happened in Ethiopia as well.[42] Traditional African political culture embodies and invites opposition in the very principle of consensus. There is an openness to being, and a readiness to expect the unexpected. Traditional African political culture teaches its people to deal with the unexpected when it arises. Africans were caught off-guard by colonization, and military juntas, causing them to suffer unimaginable losses, and the shattering of communities and ways of life. Similar to First Nations in the Americans, it was beyond their moral imagination to think that there was a world that did not affirm their humanness, and it is still the case today that they do not understand, why does the world hate them so? Theirs is a world based on a principle of sharing the joys and sorrows of life, the goods of the earth, even personal property. It is a world that affirms the supreme significance of selflessness in human relations. It affirms that humans have the right to life, and that includes the right to food. Theirs is a world based on a principle of solidarity. "There seems to be little doubt [...] that human freedom was a living reality in the democratic political culture of traditional Africa."[43]

The Euro-western world does not hate them; it selfishly ignores them. Not everyone, of course, but enough people do not see Africa's problems as their own. Enough people do not want to share their abundance of resources that they view as "theirs earned by their own hard work," and vote to selfishly limit their sharing and caring with others. The Euro-western individualistic fishing net positions Africans as "others" that we may "take care of" in limited, patronizing ways, not as equals in solidarity with us. We do not treat them as family members we are in relation with, guided by the principle of: *Feta kgomo o tshware motho* = mutual care for one another as human beings.[44]

How Anansi Turned an Ear of Corn into One Hundred Goats

Sometimes when Anansi was bored he would dream up ways to prove how clever he was. Today was such a day. Anansi went to the village Chief and asks him for an ear of corn for his dinner. The amused Chief (Nana) asks, "And what will I get in return for this ear of corn?" Anansi responds that he will repay the Chief for his kindness by turning this ear of corn into 100 goats. The Chief gave Anansi an ear of corn, wondering what he was up to now. Anansi started out the next morning, after a good breakfast, with the ear of corn in his travel sack, and he walked all day to reach a village just as night began to fall. He went to that village Chief's hut and told him that he had an ear of corn that was given to him by the Sky God, and asked if he could give him a place to rest for the night and a place to hide his sacred treasure. The Chief was honored to oblige and not only gave Anansi a place to stay and a place to hide his treasure; he threw a banquet for him in his honor. The entire village spent the evening drumming, dancing, singing, and eating and drinking to honor Anansi. Later, when they were sleeping, Anansi crept out of his hut and took the ear of corn from its hiding place and threw the corn into the chicken cage. The chickens eagerly ate up the corn. Smiling, Anansi went back to bed. In the morning he went looking for the ear of corn in its hiding place and bemoaned that someone had stolen the sacred gift. Surely you are wrong, cried the Chief, and he soon discovered that ear of corn was gone from where he had placed it for protection. Scared that the Sky God would be angry with his village, the Chief offered Anansi a bushel of corn to replace the lost ear of corn. Anansi thanked him and assured the Chief that Sky God would be grateful for his generosity, and then the spider went on his way. During the day Anansi grew tired of carrying a bushel of corn and so he traded it along the way for a chicken as one chicken is easier to carry then a bushel of corn. At the end of the day, Anansi stopped at another village and played that same trick again on the village Chief and villagers, making it look like the chicken had been stolen during the night, when all he did was pluck some of the chicken's feathers, and then put the chicken with the villagers' chickens. Again the Chief was shocked to find the chicken gone from its safe place the next morning and gave Anansi some sheep in exchange for the lost chicken so that the Sky God would not be angry at his village. On his travels the next day, while herding his sheep, Anansi came across a man with a cart, who was struggling to place a dead man into the cart, and take him back to his village where he was from. Anansi offered to take the man to his village in exchange for the cart, and to give the man with the cart his sheep, for herding sheep was tiresome work. The man agreed, and Anansi arrived at the village that evening very tired with what he told the Chief was the Sky God's son, already sleeping from their long journey. He asked the Chief for a place for both of them to rest. Again the Chief of the village was honored to take care of Anansi and the Sky God's son, and gave them a place to stay and held a banquet for them, not realizing "the son" is dead. In the morning when Anansi "discovers" he cannot waken the Sky God's son, and the villagers are not able to either with playing and singing all the songs they know as loudly as they could, they become desperate and pound on the man's chest. Anansi then accuses them of killing the man. The terrified Chief asks: what can I do to show the Sky God how sorry I am? Anansi's response, after thinking long and hard is: "one hundred goats is what is needed!"[45]

Anansi's trick only works because it counts on the village chiefs being generous, trusting, and welcoming to him. The chiefs are good to him and so are the villagers. They honor him and take care of his needs. His trick also counts on them being afraid that harm may come to their village if they don't appease the Sky God. Even though they don't believe anyone in their village would steal Anansi's various treasures, they would rather replace the missing item with something even greater than risk the Sky God's wrath. From a Euro-western perspective, Anansi is a scam artist and the African chiefs are fools, but from an African perspective, Anansi is a loveable trickster who, as small and insignificant as he may appear, is smarter than the gods and chiefs. He is not someone who should be taken for granted or ignored. He will use our character strengths and weaknesses and the principles we live by to trick us into getting what he wants. We can just imagine his own village chief laughing when Anansi comes back home with 100 goats for the ear of corn, a varietal fortune in traditional African terms.

When we travel to other continents we experience new ways of making sense of our infinite experiences. We come in contact with new cultures that have woven their own variety of spider webs to help them make sense of the booming, buzzing, and aromatic world in which they live. It is easy for misunderstandings and mishaps to occur, as happened in my stories of Ghana. I will share another story of misunderstanding that happened to me in Ethiopia in the next chapter. These misunderstandings do not need to lead to harm to the newcomer or the host in the new world. They can be insightful lessons that help us become more aware of the limitations of our own nets we have been using, and the possibilities that we need to reweave our nets to address their limitations. Too often these cross-cultural contacts have caused damage and harm to peoples' fishing nets and spider webs; they have ripped and destroyed traditions that were holding a people's way of live together. It doesn't have to be that way. There is so much wisdom to learn from other examples, if we can approach each other with respect and dignity, treat each other with kindness, generosity, and caring, and act in solidarity with each other as equals.

Conclusion

In this chapter I have explored two key threads used in the weaving of spider webs of meaning and experiences in traditional Africa, *seriti* and *ubuntu*. I have not tried to represent the rich diversity of Africa, which is an impossible task, but rather to explore key threads that traditional African cultures share in common. My sources come from various places and have diverse relationships with African philosophy as well. They include: Augustine Shutte, Mogobe Ramose, Samuel Imbo, Dion Foster, Richard Bell, and the many sources they turn to as well. I have explored the principles of *seriti*, the fundamental energy of the universe, its life force, and *ubuntu*, the fundamental connection persons have to each other, through the oral tradition of storytelling as well as through philosophical and theological scholarship, in Ananse stories from Ghana, and connected them to historical events in South Africa and Ethiopia as well.

I have also told my own stories from my travels to Ghana and Ethiopia to help us understand how our own epistemological and ontological fishing nets we inherit from birth are limited in their understanding. They affect what we catch up in our nets, or spider webs, and what we miss entirely, or misunderstand. They may help us realize our own foolishness as well as the harms our nets can cause to people in other parts of the world. My hope is that these stories and my analysis of them helps us learn more about our own limitations, what we are missing, and what harms we are causing, as they have helped me. We may also learn the strength of key relational threads Africans have used for their survival and continued resilience in a postcolonial world that can be a great source of spiritual and intellectual wisdom for us too. These principles inspire me in my personal life as well as my professional life, and I want to explore what they can mean for us in teaching our children. If we follow the *ubuntu* understanding of the cosmic and seek to preserve and maintain harmony through reaching consensus, what does that mean for our curriculum and instruction in schools? If we weave a spider web that describes our world as dynamic, attunement to be-ing, how does this change what we catch in our webs in terms of human equality, reciprocity, and solidarity, in terms of what we mean by justice and caring?

Next I turn to considering the educational implications of teaching and studenting within nets of relationality. The hope is that in describing how relational ontologies are expressed in various school models and teasing out the educational implications, this will help us better understand each other and recognize the benefits and warnings of the consequences of our various models. It is in our homes, communities, and schools, with our stories and songs, dances and music, that we weave the webs and nets we pass on to our children to help them live their lives and sustain them, until they become one with the universe again.

Notes

1. Placide Tempels, *Bantu Philosophy*, Rev. Colin King (Trans.) (Paris: Presence Africaine, 1959, 1969). Samuel Oluoch Imbo, *An Introduction to African Philosophy* (Lanham, Maryland: Rowman & Littlefield, 1998).
2. Leopold Sédar Senghor, *On African Socialism* (London: Pall Mall Press, 1964).
3. Mary Daly, *Gyn/ecology: The Metaethics of Radical Feminism* (Boston: Beacon Press, 1978/1990) and Paula Gunn Allen, *The Sacred Hoop: Recovering the Feminine in American Indian Traditions* (Boston: Beacon Press, 1986).

4. Imbo, *African Philosophy*.
5. See back cover of *Beyond Liberal Democracy in Schools: The Power of Pluralism* (New York: Teachers College Press, 2008).
6. Richard H. Bell, *Understanding African Philosophy: A Cross-cultural Approach to Classical and Contemporary Issues* (New York: Routledge, 2002).
7. Augustine Shutte, *Philosophy for Africa* (Milwaukee, Rondebosch: Marquette University Press, University of Cape Town, 1993, 1994); Mogobe Ramose, *African Philosophy through Ubuntu* (Harare, Zimbabwe: Mond Books, 1999).
8. Dion A. Forster, "African Relational Ontology, Individual Identity, and Christian Theology: An African Theological Contribution Towards an Integrated Relational Ontological Identity," *Theology*, Vol. CXIII, No. 874 (July/August, 2010): 243–253.
9. Shutte, *Philosophy for Africa*, p. 8.
10. Virginia Hamilton, Storyteller, "Spider Ananse Finds Something," *In the Beginning: Creation Stories from Around the World*. Illustrated by Barry Moser. Newberry Honor Book (San Diego, NY, London: Harcourt Brace Jovanovich, Publishers, 1988): 53–57. This Ananse spider story is from the Krachi people of Togo in West Africa.
11. Shutte, *Philosophy for Africa*, p. 8.
12. Tempels, 1959, p. 51, cited in Shutte, *Philosophy for Africa*, pp. 52, 54, 55.
13. Shutte, *Philosophy for Africa*, p. 26.
14. Ramose, *African Philosophy through Ubuntu*, p. 59.
15. See Imbo, *An Introduction to African Philosophy and Ramose, African Philosophy through Ubuntu* as examples of this defensive posture.
16. My own work was described as "A unique union of philosophy and ethnographic research" on the back book cover of *Beyond Liberal Democracy in Schools: The Power of Pluralism* (New York: Teachers College Press, 2008) by the editors of Teachers College Press.
17. Imbo, *An Introduction to African Philosophy*.
18. See, for example:Daly, *Gyn/ecology*.
19. Imbo, *An Introduction to African Philosophy*, p. 88.
20. See, for example: Gregory Cajete, *Look to the Mountain* (Durango, CO: Kivakí Press, 1994); Greg Sarris, *Mabel McKay: Weaving the Dream* (Berkeley: University of California Press, 1994); Mary Belenky, Blythe Clinchy, Nancy Goldberger, and Jill Tarule, *Women's Ways of Knowing* (New York: Basic Books, 1986); bell hooks, *Feminist Theory* (Boston: South End Press, 1984).
21. Kwame Anthony Appiah, *In My Father's House: Africa in the Philosophy of Culture* (London: Methuen, 1992). Imbo, *An Introduction to African Philosophy*.
22. Barbara J. Thayer-Bacon, *Relational "(e)pistemologies."* (New York: Peter Lang, 2003). Donna Haraway, *Simians, Cyborgs, and Women: The Reinvention of Nature* (New York: Routledge, 1991).
23. "How Anansi Won the Stories of the Sky God" from *Anansi the Trickster Spider, Volume One: Traditional African Tales retold by Lynne Garner* (ereader: Mad Moment Media LTD, 2011): loc. 237–319.
24. Shutte, *Philosophy for Africa*.
25. *Anansi the Spider: A Tale from the Ashanti*, adapted and illustrated by Gerald McDermott (New York: Henry Holt & Co., 1972).

26. Forster, "African Relational Ontology, Individual Identity, and Christian Theology," 245. Forster cites several other scholars to support his translation in his footnote 8: J. Broodryk, "Is Ubuntuism Unique?" in J. G. Malherbe (Ed.), *Decolonizing the Mind* (Pretoria: Research Unit for African Philosophy, UNISA, 1995); M. J. Bjengu, *Ubuntu: The Essence of Democracy* (Cape Town: Novalis Press, 1996); N. B. Pityana, "The Renewal of African Moral Values," in M. W. Makgoba (Ed.), *African Renaissance: The New Struggle* (Sandton: Mafube and Cape Town: Tafelberg, 1999); L. J. Teffo, *Resume of Ubuntu/Botho* (Pretoria: Ubuntu School of Philosophy, 1995).
27. Shutte, *Philosophy for Africa.*
28. Forster, "African Relational Ontology, Individual Identity, and Christian Theology," p. 245.
29. *Ibid.*, p. 247.
30. Ramose, *African Philosophy through Ubuntu*, p. 50.
31. *Ibid.*, p. 57.
32. *Ibid.*, p. 78.
33. *Ibid.*, p. 84.
34. *Ibid.*, p. 88.
35. *Ibid.*, p. 64.
36. Bell, *Understanding African Philosophy*.
37. *Ibid.*, p. 138.
38. Akalewold Eshete Kebede, "The Nature of Curriculum Practice in Primary Education: An Invitation to Curriculum Theorizing in the Ethiopian Context," unpublished dissertation (Addis Ababa University, defended January, 2016).
39. Ramose, *African Philosophy through Ubuntu*, see Chapters 6–8.
40. See, for example: Patricia Hill Collins, *Black Feminist Thought* (Boston: Unwin Hyman, 1990); Carol Gilligan, *In a Different Voice* (Cambridge, MA: Harvard University Press, 1982); Nel Noddings, *Caring* (Berkeley, CA: University of California Press, 1984).
41. Ramose, *African Philosophy through Ubuntu*, p. 138.
42. *Ibid.*, p. 140.
43. *Ibid.*, p. 145.
44. *Ibid.*, p. 142.
45. *Anansi the Trickster Spider, Volume One*, loc. 154–209.

· 6 ·

EDUCATIONAL IMPLICATIONS

Introduction

In the Introduction to this book, I presented the metaphor of a fishing net to represent the epistemological and ontological beliefs that we weave together for our children, to give meaning to their experiences and to help sustain them in their lives. I described the epistemological threads we use to help us determine what we catch up in our net as the warp threads, and our ontological threads as the weft threads. I sketched in the Introduction some of the qualities of public schools in the USA that have been passed on to us by our communities and woven into our fishing nets based on Protestant Christian ontological threads. Examples of these ontological beliefs, such as original sin, that we are born as sinners, and personal struggle on earth will be rewarded in heaven, emphasize individual effort to contain and control our impulses, and the importance of singular hard work.

In the introduction, I wondered what our schools would be like if they were based on ontological threads that were infused with a relational spirituality, holistic and wholistic in terms of nondualistic (w/holistic). What if our ontologies encouraged attunement to Being, and recognized our natural world as our kin? Instead of viewing nature in a way that is atomistic or hierarchical, what if we view Nature as relations living in connected (materially and spiritually), mutual, transactional relationships with us? How would that change our schools? What would schools look like that are based on principles of equality, reciprocity, and solidarity, rather than survival of the fittest, individual merit, and competition for more than one's share of limited resources?

In the Introduction, I sketched an example of a school model based on Indigenous ontological threads as described by Gregory Cajete in *Look to the Mountain* and *A People's Ecology*.[1] This model is one I also introduced in *Relational "(e)pistemologies."* Since writing that book in 2003, I have had the chance to spend time in several indigenous schools to help me imagine more options that develop out of relational ontologies. Cajete describes an environmental education that brings out affective, subjective, communal relations, artistic and mythical dimensions, ritual and ceremony, and what he calls *sacred ecology*. It is taught through breath, language, song, prayer, and thought. It is based on an understanding that the natural universe is imbued with life and sacredness. In this chapter, I seek to explore in more depth various models for schooling in particular and education in general, based on relational ontologies. My position is that currently we are not doing enough to teach our children in USA public schools how connected they are to each other, to their ancestors, and their indigenous neighbors, and to this living, breathing, continually changing infinite Ocean/Land/Sky/Flora and Fauna. We are not doing enough to teach our children how important their roles are as humble stewards in this reciprocal, sacred relationship. Our fishing nets need reweaving.

I begin in this chapter by summing up key ontological threads we have explored from various parts of our world, and then we will consider what kind of educational possibilities we catch up in these various nets. I will contrast the possibilities to what exists, in current school systems in the USA, based on the fishing nets used by Euro-western colonists and settlers that have undergone continual refinement. The Judeo-Christian ontology teaches our children that the Ocean is something to try to control and contain, to measure and dissect, and take from for our use, as we humans, and men in particular, have the right to use nature for our needs as we have dominion over the natural world, just as God has dominion over us. My hope is that in reweaving our fishing nets with relational ontological threads, less harm will be done to our environment and our loved ones, as well as to others' fishing nets. Our children will grow up with better understandings of their connections to other living beings, and better appreciation of their roles as stewards of their fishing nets, and of this living Earth. I also hope that by focusing on the social institution of schools, this will make it easier for us to imagine how a relational ontology changes other social institutions as well: our public work places and private home spaces, for example, as well as our health care and transportation systems, to name a few.

Summary of Relational Ontological Principles to Guide Us

William James taught us in Chapter 1 to pay attention to what spills out of our fishing nets, and what gets tangled up in them. He taught us that concepts are like nets. They are important in helping us make sense of our world, but there is more to our world than concepts can fully describe and capture. We forget to pay attention to what is *not* being captured by our concepts, and we lose those experiences in the process. There is much that spills out of the top of our conceptual net, as well as goes through the actual net, for it is not solid, but full of holes. Maybe our concepts capture more than we are trying to catch, as well as less, like when dolphins can get tangled up in fishing nets seeking to capture tuna.

James taught us to pay attention to what we do *not* capture in our nets, or capture unintentionally, and also what our nets do to others' nets. Our nets are not the only ones being used and they can get tangled up with others' nets. Some nets are not so difficult to untangle while others can receive extensive damage upon contact and will need serious mending, or even deconstructing, redesigning, and reweaving. In the meantime, serious, irrevocable harm can occur to us as our nets are what we use to sustain our lives. The kind of harm I point to is like what I described in Chapter 5 happened in South Africa to the Tutus with the arrival of Dutch and English colonizers, who eventually took over the land and claimed it as their own. Other examples of harm, described in Chapter 2, occurred to First Nations in the Americas with the arrival of the Spanish, French, Dutch, Portuguese, Russian, and English who, to varying degrees, were unable to recognize the beauty and wisdom of the sustainable nets Native Americans were weaving for their children, and they proceeded to tear them apart.

In Chapter 2 we learned that First Nations in the Americas were weaving, and still are weaving today, nets that emphasize human beings live in a constant relationship with spiritual forces and this relationship requires daily practice. They wove, and continue to weave, relational nets that are based on togetherness, synthesis, and relatedness. First Nation peoples emphasize principles of equality, reciprocity, sharing, and hospitality, and a humble awareness that the universe is much vaster than they can ever hope to comprehend completely. Thus, upon contact with explorers, their principles lead them to welcome strangers to their shores and seek to enlarge their fishing nets by learning from the newcomers. However, the newcomers came to shore with weapons of destruction, seeking material wealth, spreading unhealthy beliefs, and dangerous diseases that almost completely destroyed the indigenous peoples and their relational ontological nets. They are recovering from 500+ years of harm to their relational ontologies, slowly but surely, as the distant kin of colonizers begin to realize the harm that was caused and seek to help with the healing and recovery work. The distant kin of colonizers are starting to recognize the wisdom their indigenous neighbors had to offer, and are still willing to offer. They can show us all how to live sustainable, balanced lives.

Deleuze and Guattari taught us in Chapter 3 to pay attention to how we make our nets more stable by developing and reinforcing through policies and practice our institutions, such as higher education; but, the more stable we make them the less adaptive and flexible they are. Like deeply rooted trees and crabgrass, we need our nets to be durable and able to last over an extended period of time, to give us strength and security to help us survive storms and droughts, and not experience serious erosion of our social systems, for example. Yet, like crabgrass, we also need our nets to be able to adjust, be creative, and make new connections, as conditions continually change, and require adaption if we hope to survive.

In Chapter 4, Frank Cook described for us a universe that is incessantly changing, with the reminder that there is *no thing* that undergoes changes. We want to cling to ideas of separation, individuality, autonomy, but Buddhism calls us to pay attention to one's infinitely repeated identity and the interdependence of all phenomena. It is a cosmic ecology that is based on principles of respect, gratitude, compassion, frugality, and fair-mindedness. Buddhism encourages us to let go of our epistemological and ontological nets and float free, realizing that the very nets we work so hard to weave, reweave, and repair, so we can pass them on to our children, are the same nets that cause suffering in the world. We can end that suffering by letting go, something that is very difficult to do. There are ways to help us let go: through meditation, breathing, chanting, dancing, including physical forms of meditation such as yoga and tai chi, to name a few.

Finally, in Chapter 5 multiple African philosophers helped us understand two key relational ontological threads: *seriti* and *ubuntu*. Similar to other indigenous cultures, we learned that there is a continuous life force in the universe that is dynamic. It is the fundamental energy in the universe, and we can feel it in the Wind as it rustles our hair or pushes us around, and in the Ocean as it washes over us or slams us to the shore. We can hear it in the music of living beings buzzing, humming, calling, and crying with joy or fear. We can even taste it in the live food we eat: sweet, salty, sour, and bitter tastes in our mouths. We were reminded that no human being becomes a person, a member of a family, a village, and a community, without the help of others. It is through our participation in living with others, that we become individuals, and are embraced as members in our community. Without that welcome embrace, without generosity and compassion, without loving care, we cannot survive and grow and develop, and give back to our families, our villages and communities, our greater world.

Contrasting Principles We Currently Use

The principles described in this book and summarized previously, that people around the world have developed into various relational nets, are not principles originally or currently strongly woven into the USA's epistemological and ontological net. Although, I hasten to add, the threads in our net are continually changing and being rewoven as our population continues to grow and change. Key threads I want to draw our attention to in this section are ones that we can understand have developed from principles that were brought to the North American continent, and to other continents as well, from various parts of Europe. These principles were introduced throughout the world through European colonizers, although it is important to recognize diversity in terms of ways they were expressed (what they caught up in their nets), and how the nets have been expanded and amended to embrace more in various settings. They have adapted to differing conditions in different, specific locations.

Contrary to indigenous spiritual beliefs that humans have shared responsibilities as stewards of the land, for example, and the principle that human beings' need to find ways to live in harmony with Nature, caring for it and thanking it for what it gives us to keep us alive as well, European explorers traveled to various parts of the world seeking to claim ownership of the land

and to thank God for his gifts to them. The idea that people can own land, and later water, and now even air (in China bottled air is currently being sold), with other planets on the horizon (possible colonization of Mars), is tied to an idea that nature is here to serve men. This is a guiding thread that can be traced to Europe, and in particular to the development of science under the influence of scientists such as Sir Frances Bacon (my partner's namesake). I purposely use the term "men" in my description, as ecofeminists have made the case that the concept of "having dominion over the Earth" is a male concept that developed from early Christianity with influence from ancient Greece. Mary Daly developed this argument through the tracing of spiritual beliefs prior to Christianity and ancient Greece, to help us see their influences, and Carolyn Merchant traced the history of Euro-western science in several research projects, from an ecofeminist perspective.[2] Ecofeminists have made a strong case that men included women and children in the categories of those placed below them in a hierarchy that placed the Judeo-Christian God at the top of the heirarchy.[3] Vine Deloria, Jr. has traced this history as well from a First Nations perspective.[4]

From ancient Greece, developed over centuries in Europe, we can see influences of the belief in land ownership as it became tied to the importance of material wealth. People began to gather, maintain (one could say hoard), and inherit wealth, in the forms of land, homes, animals, crops, jewels, money, even people, generated by the labor of their families, villages, and larger communities, but also from the labor of people conquered and turned into slaves, for example. The desire for wealth can be witnessed today in the form of people competing against each other for limited resources, and believing that they deserve to keep what they have, rather than share it with others in need. Principles of hard work, and the labor of that work leading to material wealth that one has earned and therefore deserves as a reward for the hard work, have developed in the USA into the meritocratic values of competition, capitalism, and individualism, for example. As a result, we have people today who are extremely wealthy, individuals with more wealth than entire nations, and less than ten percent of human beings holding the vast majority of the Earth's wealth, while over 90 percent of human beings live in poverty or close to it.[5] The wealthy believe the myth of merit, that I deserve what I have as it is based on my hard work, and they ignore the contributions of so many others to help produce the products of wealth, as well as the sheer luck that has maybe come their way by being born into a wealthy family that afforded them so many advantages.[6]

From Judeo-Christianity, we can follow a thread that describes what happens to us, good and bad, as "God's will." "God's will" has led some people to believe they are "chosen," God's children, and for others to believe they are "saved." These spiritual beliefs in specialty, uniqueness, and having earned protection from God's wrath, have developed into judgments that others who do not include this thread in their ontologies are lacking somehow and that they are: inferior, sinners, primitive, less intelligent, backward, and even savage. Judgments of superiority have led to beliefs in manifest destiny, that it is God's will that we should have ____ (fill in the blank), for we deserve it, were used in "civilizing missions" that justified colonization. This belief in superiority has also been expressed in the value of competition, and the idea of Social Darwinism, the survival of the fittest. It can be found still today in religious beliefs that pious people have the wisdom to legislate and judge for a woman whether or not she should terminate an unwanted pregnancy, for example. Imagine a woman who is having to decide whether or not she can take care of a child, for example, a child conceived through incest or rape, or a child known to have serious health problems that will require intense care for however long that child struggles to survive. There are pious people who believe that they know what these pregnant women must do, which is to not terminate their pregnancies, without offering help for childcare or healing for the spiritual and physical wounds of violent violation of their bodies. This belief in moral superiority can be seen today in the suspicion of evil intent placed on people who do not embrace Judeo-Christian beliefs, for example, people of Muslim faith, and the belief that the pious can determine who should be allowed to immigrate to the USA, and who should be turned away as dangerous threats and potential terrorists. From a First Nations perspective, on hindsight, the Pilgrims and other early immigrants to the Americas certainly should have been turned away as dangerous to their ways of life; the "revolutionary patriots" for the establishment of a New World would be viewed as "terrorists" by those who had lived on the American continent for a long time.

Let's look at one more thread the USA seems to have inherited from Europe that was brought over with our Puritan immigrants, the Pilgrims. Our concept of time is very much forward thinking. Contrary to both African philosophy and First Nations philosophy, that treats planning in terms of three generations forward (the future), the current generation (now), and three generations past (the past), Judeo-Christian time is measured in terms of progress, toward the future (Judgment Day). Buddhists do not measure time in this linear way either; theirs is cyclical and infinitely repeating. Time is described in terms of spirals, and circling around back to a time when we were not aware of having a self, or an ego, or of perceiving ourselves as separate from others.

We, Euro-westerners, think of time as forward moving, and we equate that forward movement with progress. We tell our stories of the past as "outdated," "old-fashioned," and "regressive," just as we tend to relate to our elders, as "out-of-touch" and "conventional" or "traditional." We have developed more and more refined ways of measuring time, and more accurate timekeepers, as technology has "advanced." Where (wealthier) families used to own a family clock that would be in their home, or one timekeeper such as a pocket watch that was passed down from generation to generation as the elders passed away, the sun still helped people keep time when outdoors. Now we have cell phones we carry with us wherever we go that tell us exactly what time it is, and our cell phones adjust automatically to time changes as we travel from one time zone to another. We measure how productive we are in terms of efficient use of time, and while we used to have a pattern of time "slowing down" in warmer climates or warmer times of the year, where people had the habit of sleeping or at least resting during the heat of the day, that has changed as we have gained greater ability to control the temperature in our vehicles and buildings and turn lights on against the dark. Now we have indoor heat and air conditioning, and we can maintain a steady temperature in our homes, recreational, and work places, so that slowing down is no longer a necessity. Now we have lights that can stay on throughout the night. We go faster and work more, all in the name of "saving time." This allows us to accumulate more material wealth, but the cost is high, in terms of our physical and spiritual well-being, as well as the depletion of Earth's resources.

Belief in the value of living a sustainable life, not needing to live a life of excess or even to think it is healthy spiritually or materially to try to do that, must come from different ontological threads than the ones I describe here that the USA inherited from the Euro-west; for, these do not lead us in the direction of a balanced, restrained, and healthy lifestyle. We have managed to disconnect ourselves from *seriti*, from the fundamental energy of the universe. We have also managed to convince ourselves that we are autonomous agents, and divorce ourselves from our own families and communities. Recognizing that I am what I am because of others, *ubuntu*, originates from a relational ontological net. So does understanding that we must take care of each other including our flora and fauna brethren, and find ways to live in harmony and solidarity with each other. I turn now to exploring these contrasting nets in terms of education and schooling. First, let's look at how the above threads are taught to our children at home and in school. And then we will consider relational threads and how we can teach them, from models that can show us the ways. My examples will come from everyday, common experiences, as I seek to show through these prevalent and ordinary examples the power and influence our fishing nets have on our lives.

Educating Our Children

Home

I begin with the reminder that education is a much broader concept than schooling. Education begins when a child is born, as informal education that anyone in her community can teach her, as well as in the form of acculturation, the culture that surrounds the child and she learns through immersion. Children start to receive their family's epistemological and ontological net as soon as they are born. In fact, it is possible to argue children begin to inherit this net when they are conceived for their biological mothers who care for them in the womb, are living within particular social communities, under varying conditions of care for their maternal well-being, spiritually and materially, as well as in terms of corporeality, while they are carrying this child inside their bodies. We begin to teach our children even by the way we give birth. In many societies childbirth is treated as something natural and there is a general trust in the woman's physical ability to birth children. In other societies childbirth may be treated as a medical condition, even as a disease. In the USA, there are more children born through cesarean section than ever before, approximately one third of all babies born today, as we seem to trust medical surgery over a woman's ability to birth children vaginally. How we birth our children in turn effects how we greet them and welcome them into this world.

Once a child is delivered from her biological mother's womb, caring for the child continues within an epistemological and ontological net that our social systems have woven for us, and we have altered to fit our own beliefs and needs. We teach our children by the ways we hold them and soothe them, the songs we sing to them and the movements we make with our bodies when we rock them and dance with them, the ways we keep them dry and warm, the amount of time we spend with them and the other care-providers who spend various amounts of time with them, the ways we attend to their basic needs for food, shelter, protection from harm (or not). It is a long list of factors that come into weaving the intricate fishing net we give to our children, just looking at the day they are born, and then the first week, the first month, the first year of their lives. Before they take their first step or say their first word, they have been bathed in the sounds, smells, tastes, and touches of their family and community. Already we have been naming their experiences and giving meaning to them. And they influence us as well.

A one-year-old child already has a good amount of comprehension of her daily experiences, based on what her extended family members, neighbors, and friends have taught her. She does not take the meaning she has been given to be one of many, for she is not aware of alternatives, yet. She does not know there are multiple ways of making sense of her world, nor does she know that there are multiple worlds. She takes the one she experiences as what there is, and the net she is given to sustain her as what there is too. Children are incredibly adaptive and flexible, while at the same time they are very fragile and vulnerable. It will take many years before they can survive without care-providers' help; yet, they have been known to be able to save an adult care-provider's life even before they are able to care for themselves. It's very important that we remind ourselves how much our children already know about their world, with the help of the fishing net we give them, before they ever walk into a school building at the age of five or six.

There are documentary films made of children's first year of life, such as "Babies," that show how varied the setting can be and different the childcare practices, and yet the babies go through similar stages of development.[7] "Babies" shows four children growing up in diverse settings, two rural (Opuwo, Namibia; Bayanchandmani, Mongolia) and two urban (Tokyo, Japan; San Francisco, USA). We can see how integrated and varied their various inherited fishing nets are, and yet we see that for all four babies by the time they are one they are able to walk, feed themselves, play/explore their world, and begin to talk and interact with their family members, understanding more of their families' languages than they can say.

Babies are like little barometers; they can read their care-providers' emotions very well. They can sense when we are sad, angry, happy, excited, tired, sick, scared, bored, in pain, etc. They pay close attention to how we respond to our environment, and respond similarly, as they are also very good imitators. If we are afraid of snakes or spiders, or consider them a nuisance, they will notice this and imitate us. If we ignore these beings, or treat them with respect and praise the work they do killing mice and catching mosquitoes, they will learn to leave them alone to do their work, or maybe even take an interest in them and seek to study them. Their first reaction will not necessarily be to harm snakes or spiders, unless we teach them that. The first time my oldest child saw a bee, she was a crawling baby, and her reaction was to grab the bee, which she managed to do before I could move to stop her. Surprise on both our parts! I didn't anticipate she would try to grab the bee or that she would succeed in doing so. Much to her surprise, the bee stung her, as she squeezed it in her little fist. That hurt! As far as I know, that's the last time she did that. I soothed her and used a home remedy to draw out the stinger and help stop the pain. I also talked to her about why she should leave bees alone to do the important work they do pollinating plants. To the bee, she was a giant trying to harm him and he was just trying to protect himself. That day she may have learned some respect for insects and something about size comparison; I learned she was very observant, and faster than I anticipated, and I should be even more attentive than I was already.

If there is a loud noise, a thunder-clap, or a door slam, for example, babies may start with a cry, or they may turn to us first to see how we respond to the sound for guidance. If we are scared, they will likely be too, but if we laugh, or clap with joy, they will change their response too. Even when a child falls down, if it is not too hard of a fall, and no one is around to respond with a gasp, they will likely just pick themselves back up and go on with their exploring. Again, if we laugh, they may laugh too. When they find something new, in their exploration, they will often turn to us with a questioning expression, as if to ask, "Well, what do you think of this?" Tasting their world is an important way they initially explore it, and that can get them into all sorts of dangers. In "Babies," we see the child in Namibia, Ponijao, putting dirt in her mouth; all babies do this! Most babies enjoy getting wet and taking a bath, and Bayar, in Mongolia, has the added excitement of taking a bath, while a goat comes to drink, from the water. Many babies would love that and squeal with delight, but just as many may find it scary and cry. When we give babies food to eat, they will watch to see if we are eating it too, and if we seem to be enjoying it, and even if we are not, most likely they will try it out to see what they think of the taste. Quickly they will form their own opinions. When they find an object they want to play with and someone takes it away from them, including another baby, they will probably protest loudly. It depends on what response they get to their protests, and their own personalities, whether or not they will continue or just move on and find something else with which to play. "Babies" reminds us, we are teaching our children how to make sense of and respond to their world from the day they are born.

What are some of the ways we teach our children the ontological threads concerning progressive time, dominion over nature, and moral superiority, for example, before they go to schools for formal education? If we run our lives by a clock, and must be to work by a set time, our children learn what time means because we wake them up, instead of letting them wake up naturally on their own, and we dress and feed them, and then transport them in a car seat facing the back of a car to someone else for care for them, for example, a daycare center, so that we can be at work on time. We disappear for the day and return as the sun is setting to take them home for dinner, bathe them, and read and sing to them, and tuck them in bed for a good night's sleep, before we start the whole routine again tomorrow. If they do not have the chance to experience days and evenings where they can move at their own pace, and sleep when they are tired and wake when they are done resting, eat when they are hungry, and play without having to stop to fit another's schedule, they will not know about time as cyclical, for example. They will know about time that progresses from work days to rest days, and is measured by some powerful external force called a "clock."

How we spend time with our children matters, in terms of sharing with them our joys and wonders, as well as our fears and sorrows. If we are uncomfortable outdoors and do not seek to take them on walks in woods, or camping in a field or at the beach, or swimming in a lake or river, or even a swimming pool, they will probably not be comfortable outdoors as easily too. My parents hated camping, and never took me camping as a result, but they did send me to Girl Scout camp in the summers where I learned to love camping and sleeping under the stars, as well as hiking and canoeing, for example. If we have no plants in our homes and no gardens, our children will not learn from their surroundings that plants give us beauty and joy, pleasant smelling aromas and flavor for our food, as well as tasty food to eat, for example. They also will not learn easily and directly that plants require tending to, such as watering, and protection from sunlight, and not to pull off their leaves or break their branches as that will harm the plants' ability to grow and thrive.

We teach our children to say thank you for their food to the animals that gave their lives so we may eat, and the farmers that grew our food, by modeling this for them every time we pause and say thank you, prior to eating. They will learn to pause too, as they are watching us and imitating us, every time we eat. If we thank God for these blessings before us, instead of the animals, or the farmers, or Mother Earth, that is the ontological net we give our children. If we complain every time we see a homeless person, why don't they get a job? Or we ignore those in need asking for help, we are teaching our children lessons of moral superiority. Whatever church we take our children to on Sundays, or mosques on Fridays, or temples on Saturday, that is another important opportunity to teach them our ways of life. We teach them what we do with our extra resources by how we exchange gifts, for example, at holiday times or their birthdays, and the kinds of gifts we give. Do we limit the amount we give to family members so that we may give to others in need as well, or make gifts for each other, or give to excess, as a measure of our love? If we give to donation plates at church, or drop coins in peoples outstretched hands, musician's hats or instrument cases, or buy weekly newspapers from the homeless, or take our children with us to work in homeless shelters cooking a monthly meal for them, or ask our children to pass on their clothes and toys they have outgrown to other children in need, these are all ways we model for our children daily feelings of moral superiority, or how we show care for others who are our kin.

Schools have played a secondary role to home and the extended community in the early years of a child's life, historically. However, they do have a strong influence as well and their level of influence continues to evolve as children spend more time in school settings and less time with their extended family members. Let's consider ways we currently teach children in USA schools, that reflect some of our current values, as described previously, and in contrast we will consider how we could be reweaving for them threads of relationality. Remember, I seek to give examples that are everyday, common experiences in USA public schools, to show, through their ordinariness, the level of influence they have on our lives.

Schools

When I was a young child in the late 1950s, children started school between the ages of five to eight in the USA. It was not required by law to begin school until the age of eight in many states even when my children were starting school in the 1980s, and it was not considered unusual for a child to delay enrolling in school. In fact, for many children, parents were advised to delay their start in school until their child had more time to mature. The expectation was that school requires a child to sit still in a desk for long periods of time and many young children are physically not yet able to do that. Around the world children enroll in schools at various ages, depending on availability, access, family needs, resources, valued importance, children's health, and many factors. The amount of time I spent in school was around three hours as a five-year-old, and up to six hours in secondary/high school. The number of days I spent in school was around 150 out of a year (365 days).

In today's world, the age children enter school is younger, overall, and more children are beginning "school" as babies, in daycare facilities, prior to turning one year old. When I was young I spent more time outside of school buildings than in them, and my "outside of school" time was less structured than it is for many children today as well. My granddaughters were in daycare by three to six months of age, and they are there from eight am to four or five pm year-round. They are at home only for about three hours/day when they are awake, and on the weekends. They are not yet school age but are already accustomed to "going to school." The boundaries between home and school have changed significantly in the USA in my lifetime. These changes are occurring worldwide, as more parents and extended childcare providers must, or choose to, work in ways to support themselves that do not allow inclusion of children possible. Schools and other childcare facilities continue to extend their hours to help meet families' needs. As schools, including daycares, before and after school care facilities, extend their time with children, they also extend their influence. What are examples of threads they currently teach our children and grandchildren?

Linear, progressive time, as a key ontological thread we weave in the USA, is even more pervasive for today's children than when I was a child. It is not just the extra hours each day, and days each year that children spend in school, it is also the way we manage time when they are in school. Teachers set up their day around clocks, even at the preschool level and in daycare facilities, with a set time for snack (morning and afternoon), recess (morning and afternoon), circle time, play time, lunch, nap time, story time. Even bathroom time is scheduled into children's days. If John Calvin (1509–1564) were alive today, he would be quite pleased to see how closely our schools resemble what he recommended so long ago during the Protestant Reformation.[8] Calvin made plans for a school that would guide the education of children, a grammar school called the *collège*, and an advanced school called the *acadèmie*. Calvin's school was designed to have the students' daily activities scheduled from the moment they awoke until they went to sleep in the evening, so that they would not be tempted to get into trouble. Sunday was a day to spend in church, and under the watchful eyes of the church elders. The belief was that "idle hands are the devil's workshop," and it was the job of teachers and church elders to guide the children and oversee their days/nights to make sure they were not led astray. "Free time" was not a concept viewed positively by Calvin; it was an enemy to be eliminated.

In USA schools, today we have bells, whistles, and alarms that tell us when we may enter and leave the building, when the day begins and ends, when to move from one subject to another, or from one room to another for a different class with a different teacher, when to go outside for recess and when to come back in (if we are lucky enough to still have recess), when to line up to go to the bathroom, or to lunch (which may be for only 20 minutes), or to catch the bus home. We teach our children daily about time.

Related to the issue of time, as linear and progressive, we also teach children in schools about work/labor. Again, I am extending school age down to preschool (three-to-six-year-olds), and worrying that it has extended down to even daycare (infants–three-year-olds). The Protestant Reformation took away the power of guidance and forgiveness for our sins from priests and put it in each individual's hands. I must work hard on earth in order to hope to be allowed into heaven on Judgment Day. School used to be open to only those seeking to become priests or other religious scholars, or for the wealthy who could hire tutors for their children (usually their sons), but after the Protestant Reformation school became open to more and more children. Commoners were encouraged to learn how to read so that they could read the Bible themselves and seek their own salvation. Within five years of Calvin's school opening, there were 1,200 students in the grammar school and 300 in the advanced school.

In school, we teach children to "work hard" and "not waste time" on idle talk with other children, or play. We give them tasks (assignments, activities) and make sure they complete these tasks by a set time. If they do not complete the tasks they are punished, by taking away "free time" (e.g., recess) and giving them more work. "Work" often comes in the form of copying from a board (or overhead, or PowerPoint, or computer screen) or doing worksheets (or workbooks, textbooks, or ereaders). If the children do manage to complete their assigned tasks, they are rewarded, often with extrinsic rewards such as stickers, gold stars, treats, points, grades, maybe even a party for a big assignment completion. We "count" the children's work, by assessing it and giving feedback about its quality, and return it to them, or often we just dispose of it (or their families do). From a Protestant Reformation perspective in Calvin's time and during early pioneer development, we taught our children to work hard, and that hard work in this world will count in the next world, on Judgment

Day. Today the lesson of working hard is not necessarily framed for reward in heaven; instead it is framed for economical reward in *this* lifetime here on earth. Going to school and working hard, doing all of one's assignments in a timely manner and submitting them for evaluation, as well as going home to do more assignments in the evenings (homework), will help our children qualify for jobs where they can work hard to be able to receive a paycheck as their reward, and raise the quality of their lives, materially, if not spiritually.

For young children, grades are meaningless. We have to teach them what they mean and to value them. Young children will willingly share their stickers and gold stars with other children who are their friends, and children who look sad because they did not earn a gold star or sticker. We have to teach them to horde their external rewards and compete with each other, instead of collaborating and sharing. It is true; two-year-olds want things for themselves and can have a hard time sharing with others. Mine! They will fight with other children over objects of desire and try to keep the object to themselves. But they are easy to distract with another object, and easily appeased with both children receiving the same or similar items. It's not unusual for young children to forget about something they were in tears over just a short while ago. It is not unusual for children with special needs such as children with Down Syndrome to not ever understand the meaning and value we place in grades. What they can understand much more easily is our facial expressions, our joy or disappointment in the work they accomplish or are not able to do.

Children also have to be taught to view themselves as morally superior to other children, due to their merit of some kind or other in regards to their work. They will not necessarily notice how others are doing in comparison to themselves unless we draw it to their attention. Even if they do notice, for example, that another child is better able to build blocks, or color a picture, they will not conclude from that child's talent that the child is "better than them" unless they are taught this concept. We teach children in school to compare themselves to each other and judge one to be of higher merit than another. Maybe we give them more attention and praise, we notice their work and give them more rewards, or we don't. Children get sifted and sorted by our assessments of their skills and talents, or it could be that we value their looks: they are clean, have blue eyes, have a lighter skin color, or blond hair, for example. Their parents dress them in cute clothes, or style their hair, for example. Or we give them more attention than other children in the school because of their parents' higher social status and/or power. Maybe we enjoy certain children's personalities more than others, because they smile a lot, or can sit still longer, or do not demand too much of us. For many reasons, we respond to children in schools differently and sort them into different academic and/or behavior groupings, and place them with others perceived to be learning and maturing at the same pace, for example. In the process, we teach them to view themselves as morally superior to others and give them credit for earning our praises. Thus, the myth of merit is created and woven into our children's fishing nets.

What about how we teach children in school to view nature? One of the most powerful forms of instruction we use for school children is to separate them from nature. We bring them inside, and keep them in climate-controlled buildings. By removing them from the natural world and placing them in artificial settings called "schools," we teach them to feel uncomfortable and unfamiliar with their natural surroundings. When we do let them go outside to play, we often scold them when they get dirty, even punish them by making them come inside, and lose their "outdoor privileges." Or, we draw attention to them but in ways that embarrass and demean them by doing something like scrubbing them down and insisting they change their clothes. We may even isolate them from the other children and put them in "time out."

It is becoming more difficult to find schools that teach children about the nature that surrounds them, in their natural settings. Mainly our children are learning about nature from books and films, and observations in aquariums or zoos, much more indirectly than they used to be able to learn through direct experiences. The "direct experiences" they receive now are by using tools such as magnifying glasses, microscopes, and dissecting knives, to look at nature stained and magnified and placed on a slide or in a petri dish, if they are fortunate enough to have that kind of equipment. Maybe they have the chance to take a field trip to a museum that has engaging activities and tools for making observations. Then we assess them through their lab reports and with a multiple-choice test to see what they have learned. And do not forget, our children are spending more and more of their time in school spaces learning about nature in these kinds of ways.

When I was earning my masters degree in curriculum and instruction, while teaching fulltime as an elementary Montessori teacher, we were assigned to read *The Saber-Tooth Curriculum.*[9] It is written as a conversation (series of lectures) taking place in a Mexican bar in Tijuana, between a former professor and a bartender. The former professor explains why he has quit teaching, as the curriculum has become more and more removed from the world of living beings. Then he tells a story of the development of curriculum and instruction theories as taught to Paleolithic children that ends with the last living saber-tooth tiger being placed in a cage in the classroom so that the students can learn what a real tiger is like. It is a humorous story that helps us realize how disconnected our curriculum and methods of instruction have become from "the real world" outside of the classroom and school building. Then I learned that *The Saber-Tooth Curriculum* was originally published in 1939. I was reading this book in the 1980s, 50 years later, and we were still doing what the author described, and are still doing it today. The thread in our ontological fishing net that disconnects us from the natural world is stronger today than in 1939 when an author was able to use wit, and wisdom to help us understand the illogical, disengaged, disconnected ways we were teaching children about their natural world.

Hopefully, I have described enough from common, ordinary experiences in USA schools, to help us understand how we pass on to our children the key ontological threads that we weave for them and teach them to apply, as we seek to help them make sense of their experiences. The threads not only help them give meaning to their world, but also these threads help determine what experiences they catch up in their fishing nets, versus what spills out through the net and over the top. We also teach them what to throw away, that we do not want them to catch in their nets. Now let's turn to consider different lessons taught in alternative schools in the USA and other parts of the world, which can serve for us as relational counter examples to our own Euro-western ontologies.

Contrasting Examples

We who have been raised to use Euro-western epistemological and ontological nets with the kind of strong daily influences I describe previously at home as well as at school (and I have not discussed at all other influences in our lives such as church and media), may have trouble imagining other possibilities for our schools and other social institutions like our homes and health care systems. It is very difficult to become aware of the strongly woven threads of our net; they are so much a part of our daily lives. I have found that exposing myself to diverse alternative ways of living and being has been the best way to help me become aware of my own way of being. With that awareness comes the possibility to evaluate those threads for their beauty and inspiration, strength and durability, flexibility and adaptability, and sustainability, for example, as well as for their harmful qualities such as weakness, rigidity, ugliness, and stingy meanness. If we can critique our basic threads then we can work on repairing, replacing, and reweaving them. If we can imagine other possibilities, we can even create anew, with the help of others who share our visions and values. I am arguing that we must try to reweave our ontological threads with relational threads for the sake of the well-being of our children, their children, and their children's children as well as our own lives, our parents, grandparents, and great-grandparents lives on this Earth.

I have described ontologies that emphasize the interdependence and spirituality of all living beings in the previous chapters. The relational ontologies included in this book describe the universe as living, a fundamental energy that is continuous and dynamic. They express values of respect, equality, and solidarity, gratitude, fair-mindedness, and compassion, frugality, sharing and generosity, hospitality, love, and forgiveness. What kind of social structures can we design to help support these values for our children, and help them grow and thrive? My task in this last section is to help us consider various possibilities. I turn to examples from my own teaching experiences as a Montessori teacher, as well as observations and stories from various schools I have visited around the world or have read about through scholarship. They will help us imagine ways to reweave and make room for our children's efforts and imaginations as well.

Many parents find themselves in the situation where they cannot find schools that embrace the values they are trying to teach their children. At home, they may have a significant level of control when their children are very young for they can live in places where their children are surrounded by others who support their vision and the meanings they wish to give to their children of this world. They can live in compounds, villages, and small towns, in communes, kibbutzim, and communities with other extended family members, and friends, and as a village they can raise their children. But, it is next to impossible to keep outside influences at bay for children as they expand their explorations and are exposed to more diverse values. Families can hope to teach their children to live simple, frugal lives full of generosity and sharing, for example, but then their children have to go to school (by law) and are exposed to other values through the media, for example (television, radio, movies, etc.). In the USA, it is almost impossible for children to grow up without exposure to marketing efforts to make them desire material wealth, with a linked promise of happiness, for example.

Some families solve this problem of incongruity of values by seeking to maintain control as long as they can and do not enroll their children in state-run schools, but instead educate their children at home. Still, they must find ways to tackle influences that come through the media, popular culture, and the internet, for example. I did not own a television for the first 12 years of my parenting, hoping to soften the influences of the media on my children and encourage them to play outside more, but it only made them more curious about what they were missing that their friends in the neighborhood were watching. They grew up and as adults watched the television shows they missed as children. However, by then they were armed with as much protection as I could offer. They had learned how to critique influences they may not want to absorb and seek alternative possibilities. They had learned much from exploring the world around them and reading about other worlds beyond their neighborhood and community. They had learned how to imagine other ways of being and weave a net with values they embraced that could sustain them.

Like many parents who must work for a living, I was not able to home-school my children, nor did I think that was a good idea for fear it would isolate them from other children and the important skills they develop by befriending others not like them. My children were growing up in a single-parent home in a country that values autonomy, individual choice, and freedom and had developed a model for (white) families that was atomistic, and individualized, the nuclear, heterosexual family: one mother and father and a few children, no extended family members to help. Like many families that did not fit that nuclear family model represented throughout the 1950s television, we had to create another model that worked better for us. In today's world less than 50 percent of families in the USA fit that nuclear family model, and we have a better awareness of the need to have many people involved in supporting families and helping to do elder and childcare work. As a single mother with no extended family living nearby, I had to create my own support system with friends who also needed help raising their children, and we formed a babysitting co-op, food co-op, and an alternative school for our children. We were young parents with little income raising children in the 1980s.

I had the good fortune of being able to find a way to bring home and school values together, by helping to grow a school that supported the values I was trying to teach my children at home, *The Growing Concern*. This little Montessori school, which still exists, gave me the village I needed to raise my children.[10] As the African concept, *ubuntu*, so clearly describes, it truly takes a village to raise a child. One parent cannot do it alone.

While there are significant varieties of Montessori schools for they are not protected by copyright law and anyone can hang up a sign and call their school a Montessori school, there are general principles she established in her pedagogy that all licensed schools with trained/certified Montessori teachers try to follow. One is that the children in Montessori schools are allowed to work at their own pace throughout the day as much as possible. It is important that they be allowed to complete their own cycles of concentration with the learning materials without others interrupting them, even at the preschool age-level. Montessori wisely labeled the activities preschool-aged children chose to do "work," instead of "play," so that adults would see the children's tasks as meaningful and important and take them seriously. That was a significant thread she developed in her educational net, as it captured and helped people see what before had been falling through the holes of their nets, unnoticed. She insisted that children have extended periods of time that are not interrupted by other activities, so that they could work at their pace, not the adults' pace. Consequently, a typical Montessori school daily schedule will have extended open time slots (up to three hours), with music and art included as part of the curriculum and outdoor physical activity included around lunch time, for example, and/or the end of the day.

Not only can children work at their own pace in Montessori schools, but also they can eat a snack whenever they want, rest if they need to, and use the restroom as needed. Their essential physical needs are for them to regulate, not for adults to tell them when they have permission to do these basic tasks. Food preparation is available as "practical life work" that is on the shelves in the classroom kitchen area every day, for example. They can use a bathroom whenever they need to as long as one is available. Usually at the preschool-level restrooms are in the classroom. In my elementary school, the restrooms were down the hall and the children took themselves there with a bathroom pass whenever they needed to, one at a time. They can move around the classroom space, deciding if they want to work in a desk, at a table, on a rug, even possibly on a loft if their classroom has this. No child is required to sit in a desk for extended periods of time, even in the elementary classrooms. Children are able to function more to their internal rhythms than to someone else's external "clock" and to move to fit their own physical needs.

If at all possible, Montessori classrooms are designed to be open to the outdoors. Our school originally was a rented space in a former public school that had a backyard area for recess and some science curriculum, but the children could not go outside easily as they had to cross a parking lot to get to the grass area. An adult had to go with the children to make sure they were safe. However, a few years after establishing our school, the staff were able to purchase property that connected to protected park land, and that opened up a much more conducive space for extending the inside classroom space outdoors. Nature no longer had to be intentionally brought in, or children taken out under adult supervision, but the doors could be opened to extend the classroom to a patio area where the children could work at portable tables and easels, for example, and the study of geographic shapes such as mountains, rivers, capes, and bays could be done in sand boxes where water could be easily poured. The children were (and still are) able to learn about Nature while surrounded by it, and study the seasons, for example, as they experience them, watching plants bud, flower, and turn to seed, and the leaves grow, change color, and fall. They may observe deer as they graze in the meadow outside their classroom window, chart changing weather patterns, and measure rainwater as part of water-cycle studies, etc. My elementary class celebrated the changing seasons with an outdoor lesson that marked off the earth's elliptical orbit around the sun and noted where the earth was located for autumnal equinox and vernal equinox, for example. If we want children to learn how to live in a sustainable world, understand their stewardship roles, and experience the spiritual as well as material well-being of kinship with Nature, we need to give children direct, diverse experiences in that natural world that surrounds them.

In my elementary-age Montessori classroom, the children were never given extrinsic rewards for their work, such as gold stars, stickers, special food, grades, points, or check marks on a chart. Another important principle for Montessori is to trust that children want to learn. Their reward for working on a material is the joy of being able to complete the work. Since the children choose their own work, and everything in the classroom is a learning material that, once they have been shown how to use, they can choose, then the teacher's role changes dramatically from having to worry about classroom management and maintaining authority to observing what the children choose to do, and what they avoid. Theirs becomes a task of developing more curricula to meet the diverse needs of the students. The reward for the children is intrinsic, the joy of learning. Again, the children work at their own pace as much as possible, not based on a teacher's clock, and they choose what work they want to do, and how often.

Another important issue that Montessori addressed with the relational education net she wove is the issue of causing some children to feel superior, or chosen, or deserving of merit, by how the students are positioned in relation to each other. We learned previously how American public schools sift and sort children into different classes by age and ability level, and position them in tracks so that some are perceived to be smarter and more talented than others. There are no tracks in a Montessori classroom. Everyone works at their own pace in terms of mastery of the curricula and they are not compared to others in their classroom. They are only compared to themselves. The classrooms typically have three ages together in one room, so that preschool classrooms will have three-to-six-year-olds, lower elementary classrooms will have six-to-nine-year-olds, and upper elementary classrooms will have nine-to-twelve-year-olds. Sometimes this will vary depending on the number of children enrolled that particular year in the school, but I always had at least three ages together, and sometimes four. In multiaged classrooms there are multiability levels as well.

The general principle is that children are shown work that matches their skill level, and their interests, and once they have mastered that material, are able to be teachers and show that work to others. They are taught to pay attention to their own learning. Every person in the classroom is positioned as a potential teacher, and in a multiaged classroom space there are all sorts of opportunities for all the children to also be teachers and help other children. This model of education encourages children to learn how to work well with others and collaborate with others as peer tutors, instead of comparing themselves to others and competing against their classmates for a teacher's attention and external rewards. The children are encouraged to develop relationships of equality, reciprocity, and solidarity.

I have observed public schools on the Navajo (Diné) Reservation with similar structures and goals intact to what I describe with Montessori schools.[11] In one kindergarten–second grade primary school, I observed the teachers had a choice of either teaching in multiaged classrooms with children ages five to seven, or teaching in a "looping" structure where they stayed with the same class of five-year-olds through second grade (age seven). Both models were offered as ways to give the young children a great deal of support from their teacher and classmates, to help them open up to learning in school, rather than resist it out of fear. This school is very aware that the Euro-western curriculum in the public schools is different from what most of the children are exposed to at home and will take more time and support to learn. The children are not necessarily growing up in homes (hogans) surrounded by literary adults, especially for the elders, as the Navajo (Diné) language was only put into written form in the 1930s, printed as a dictionary in 1943. However, they also know deeply the parental values and the tribal values, the relational fishing net the clans give to their young, as most of the teachers today working in Diné Primary are from the same clans and tribal nation as the children, as is the principal of the school. They seek to help the children become bilingual and bicultural without causing harm to the original fishing nets their extended families gave them. They seek to help the children expand their nets, and extend them, not tear them apart with deficit theories of what they lack or are incapable of doing.

While I was observing in Diné Primary, I was privileged to attend a teachers meeting where two representatives of a major book publishing company presented their set of science books to the teachers.[12] The teachers looked carefully through the books, including looking at the pictures, as they listened politely to the sales representatives. Then they pointed out to the representatives that there were no pictures of Native Americans in the books and no representation of Native American cultural values. There were also no images of the kind of flora and fauna the children know so well, and no discussion of Nature as the Navajos present this to their children. The sales representatives were surprised to find in searching themselves that the teachers were correct, Native American students were not included in these beautiful science textbooks' pictures, and their cultural beliefs were not included in the science curriculum, even though this textbook publishing company prides itself on producing multicultural curriculum. The teachers were not surprised; they have run into this issue again and again. They voted to only buy one set of these science books, which would be available as a resource for the teachers to use (or not), but would not be on the shelves in their classrooms. The students would not need to see that they were not reflected in the images and they would not need to know that their culture was not reflected in the books as well. The teachers' votes were to affirm: that is a deficit lesson to which they do not need to expose the children.

The teachers on the Navajo Reservation, in all their schools, find they have to design their own curriculum if they want to introduce the children to science in a way that reflects indigenous values. For example, Rough Rock teachers created a beautiful text titled *Between Sacred Mountains* which is illustrated by Navajo artists and shows what the way of life was like on the Reservation prior to Euro-western contact, and postcontact.[13] Sheep and horses were brought to the Southwest by the Spanish explorers and became part of the Navajo way of life. In fact, the sheep were (and still are) considered sacred family members. Each child is given a sheep and learns how to tend to their sheep. The Navajos are famous for their abilities as shepherds, as well as for their sheep's wool, and for the Navajo rugs they make from the wool. The sheep contribute significantly to family incomes.

The Navajos developed a pastoralist way of life that allowed them to graze their livestock without overgrazing the land. However, the USA federal government decided the Navajos were overgrazing their land and causing soil erosion, and feared the erosion would harm the Hoover Dam they wanted to build (1931–1936). Based on little evidence, they exterminated over 80 percent of the Navajos' sheep, with the families there to watch this slaughter. The Navajos are still recovering from the trauma this caused their families and way of life, and the land has not recovered yet, as well. It turns out the sheep were actually helping prevent the land from eroding into the Colorado River, and their grazing was helping maintain healthy plants that have now been replaced by inedible weeds. The plant life has changed as a result of the slaughter of their sheep by the USA Army during the 1920s–1930s. This is a powerful example of the kind of recovery work Diné families and teachers are doing together, to help them heal from Euro-western rips and tears to their relational ontological nets.

Let me share a story from Ethiopia, which illustrates how curriculum and instruction become translated into schools and how home and established traditional ontologies affect this. The premise of this research is based on the historical process that created Ethiopia as a multiethnic empire state at the dawn of the twentieth century and the modernization policy pursued during Haile Selassie I and Derg regimes described in Chapter 5. Post-1991 Ethiopia, at least rhetorically embraced democratization of state and society. The study researches how democratization of education was addressed by two self-autonomous regional states and as they attempt to establish "student-centered curriculum and pedagogy" in their respective primary schools.

Story Seven

Before arriving in Ethiopia I was sent a dissertation to read, and review, that I might ask questions of the doctoral student in his oral defense, upon my arrival. The topic was of interest to me, curriculum reform. The abstract promised to inform me about current practices in primary education in Ethiopia. The title of this dissertation is: *The Nature of Curriculum Practice in Primary Education: An Invitation to Curriculum Theorizing in the Ethiopian Context* by Akalewold Eshete Kebede.[14] I read a ten-chapter dissertation about curriculum reform that I thought I understood. It cited many Euro-western scholars whose work I know quite well, have cited in my own research projects, and often have my students read and discuss in my classrooms. The focus of the curriculum reform effort was on making the curriculum more "child-centered" at the primary level. It was only as I finished the dissertation, near the end of its ten chapter, that I realized I was translating the concept "child-centered" curriculum and instruction from within my Euro-western epistemological and ontological net, and that what I thought was the meaning of that concept was not correct, from an Ethiopian perspective. I may know the scholars being cited but I did not know what the people of Ethiopia took "child centered" curriculum and instruction to mean.

In Euro-western terms, "child-centered curriculum" means a curriculum that is based on getting to know the individual child and what her interests are, and then designing the curriculum so that it taps into the child's individual interests. It is based on an individualistic view of children and their unique needs. In Ethiopia "child-centered curriculum" has been translated to mean the prototype student textbooks written by the Federal ministry (with the help of international and local textbook industry) and self-autonomous regional states are allowed to adapt them to the culture of their constituent language groups (called nation, nationalities, and people). In order to make the same material for the various language groups in the country, adaptation is taken as basically to mean translation of the materials into students' home languages by taking some examples from their culture, topography and peoples, plant and animal names.

Similarly, "child-centered pedagogy" has been translated to mean dividing up students in a classroom into groups of five (commonly called one to five groups, one clever, two averages. and three weak students), with the strongest student being assigned the leader role. This group is the basic unit of classrooms as teachers use them during instruction, when they set up group work, and also in their "spare time" as study groups. Due to the declining quality of education as revealed by poor achievement results, teachers are expected to "support" this group by giving weekly study questions. Teachers then help leaders study these questions and later on the leader teaches the two average students what the teacher taught him, and then the two average students teach the three-weak students in the group. There is an established hierarchy in the groups, with the leaders not only responsible for academic matters, but also responsible for controlling the other students in their group in terms of monitoring students attendance, discipline, tardiness, homework done, etc. The classroom management is done now at three levels: by the general overview of the teacher, by the selected monitors at the classroom level, and by the leaders at the group level, with the grouping and tracking of students within each group determined by the teachers. The content and orientation of discipline protocols are essentially the same as before. Teacher directed, highly structured lessons are still taken as normal and are unchallenged. The textbook is still taken as the source of knowledge, and relevance or connection to students' lives is not attempted.

What has changed is the teaching method, in that before teachers stood in the front of the room and presented all the lessons and now the students meet in their groups after the teacher has instructed the whole class or leaders of the groups to their weekly set questions, and the leaders then present the instructing from within their groups. It is "child-centered" curriculum and instruction but it means something completely different than what I thought it did! The "One-to-Five Groups" help the large classrooms of 50 to 60 students be controlled, and are a way of offering support and help to students, so that hopefully more students' needs will be met. Leaders help/explain, and average students do so as well, and the weak students' roles are to study and receive help. The hope is that this method of instruction will allow more students to receive an education in terms of achieving higher marks and fewer students will drop out of school, without having to hire more teachers, which they cannot afford to do. What the government has been discovering is that as they make education universally available, the quality of the education is diminishing. New reform efforts seek to address the quality issue. However, content and orientation of discipline protocols are essentially the same.

Kebede explains how the "One to Five Groups" model reinforces how power and authority work in the school system, family, and society in general. It is a hierarchical conception of authority that positions teachers as managers and passive implementers of expert designs. Kebede argues that this model further privileges the group leaders and marginalizes the average and weak students. He finds it is a good description of the society's view of children as flowers, or future seeds, and the school's role as cultural transmission. He explains Ethiopian cultural tradition as acceptance of hierarchy as legitimate social order, and that knowledge should not be questioned or new knowledge searched for. Ethiopian acceptance of authority goes for the leader (God given) and the family as well, which is based on a patriarchal model. Children are taught obedience and conformity to the dictates of parents and elders. Individual initiative and inquisitiveness are considered defects and are discouraged. There are evil consequences for curiosity, and human agency is actively discouraged. Kebede's central finding is that the schools are a reflection of life in contemporary Ethiopian society. Post-1991 curriculum in Ethiopia has not departed from the past; it is just more rationalized.

My point with this last example is to help us understand that we can change the terms we use to describe our curriculum but that does not mean we change the curriculum or our methods of instruction significantly. It does not change our ontology, necessarily. How we teach our children and what we teach them are based on deep-seeded ways we make sense of our world, what criteria we use to help us determine what counts as knowledge, and how we respond to our infinite world in terms of basic categories of Being. We begin to give our children the net they will use to catch up from this infinite world their experiences as soon as they are born, and it takes a lifetime to become aware of those deep influences, and amend them if we so desire. We need to become aware of our basic threads, before we can critique them, and work on repairing or replacing them, or maybe we decide we should let them be. My hope is that the few examples I offer here are enough to help us imagine new possibilities, and consider the importance of trying to reweave our ontological threads with relationality.

Schools are one example of social institutions and families are another. They are powerful examples that are central to our lives and are important to consider, if we seek to make changes to our fishing net. We do have other social institutions though that we could explore, such as health care, transportation, and economic systems. We have newer systems we should consider, such as the media's internet web. These are all important to consider, but they are beyond the scope of this book and my expertise. As a philosopher of education, my work is done here. I look forward to discovering what others may do, in applying *relationality* to these other threads.

Conclusion

In this text, I developed several differing examples of "nets" to help us understand the philosophical concept of *ontology* and the powerful role ontology plays in our lives, including Indra's Net, rhizomes in the form of crabgrass, and spider webs. We considered problems with nets in terms of what spills out of them and what gets tangled up in them, and how to make them adaptive and flexible. We considered relationality in terms of interdependence of all phenomena (*cosmic ecology*), and how Buddhism helps us understand that what spills out of our nets is a symbol of incessant change and flux that is the infinite universe. There is *no thing* that undergoes the changes. Buddhism seeks to help us become aware of the fishing nets we have inherited so that we can learn how to let go of them, and by doing so end suffering.

I did not write this book for other philosophers whose work focuses on traditional ontology, as likely they will be disappointed by its lack of depth of anticipated philosophical discussion. I also did not write this book for a particular religious audience, as it is not written from a particular religious perspective, but certainly with spirituality in mind. I defined ontology and spirituality as equivalent concepts about our basic categories of Being. As a philosopher of education, I sought to describe *relational ontologies* with parents and school teachers, key educators, in mind. I wanted to use a language that is accessible to nonprofessional philosophers and examples that can be related to by all of us involved in the very important work of educating our children and helping them learn how to survive, even thrive, in their various communities. Those of us tasked with helping our young make sense of their daily experiences through the language and customs we teach them and the behaviors we model for them as we go through our daily lives, we are giving our children an ontological and epistemological net to help sustain them, until they able to return to the infinite Ocean/Sky/Natural World from which they came.

Much of this net we give our children, the future generation, was woven for us by our elders, the past generations, but it also contains threads we contribute, reweavings we make for them, as the current generation. My hope with this project is that I have made it easier for us to see threads in the epistemological and ontological nets we cannot help but use in our daily lives, and understand their influences. I hope we can pay closer attention and notice what all is spilling out of our nets, and through our nets, and even what we are catching in our nets that we do not mean to catch. We can be grateful for the life-sustaining nets our ancestors have woven for us, and seek to help maintain them for future generations. But, we must try to notice the harms they cause as well, and seek to repair these.

I have not argued for a particular ontological fishing net, in fact I have offered diverse examples for us to consider in an effort to encourage us to recognize there are multiple ways of describing our world. I do not think there is one best way, nor do I think it is a goal we should even seek to achieve. I have argued that our nets are always limited, there is always more in this infinite world of experience then we can ever hope to catch up with our concepts. Our nets can never hope to capture all, that is the definition of infinity. We can only achieve infinity if we let go of our nets altogether and become one with the universe, as Buddhism teaches us. Meanwhile, the best we can hope for is to learn from each other how to be good stewards of our various fishing nets and recognize their flaws and seek to repair them. We can learn how to adapt our fishing nets and improve upon them, if we are able to recognize that there are limitations as well as multiple ways of making sense of our world. That is my hope. I sought in this book to describe weft threads of nondualistic relational ontologies and help us imagine various possibilities for educating our children by relying on such weft threads, ones that encourage attunement to Being, instead of ones we have inherited that are causing us so much harm.

Notes

1. Gregory Cajete, *Look to the Mountain* (Durango, CO: Kivakí Press, 1994); Gregory Cajete, *A People's Ecology* (Santa Fe, NM: Clear Light Publishers, 2000).
2. Mary Daly, *Gyn/ecology* (Boston: Beacon Press, 1978, 1990); Carolyn Merchant, *The Death of Nature* (San Francisco: Harper and Row, 1980); Carolyn Merchant, "Ecofeminism and Feminist Theory," in Irene Diamond and Gloria F. Orenstein (Eds.), *Reweaving the World: The Emergence of Ecofeminism* (San Francisco: Sierra Club Books, 1990): 100–105; Carolyn Merchant, *Radical Ecology: The Search for a Livable World* (New York: Routledge, 1992).
3. See, for example: Ynestra King, "What is ecofeminism?" *The Nation*, 245(20) (1987): 730–732; Ynestra King, "The Ecology of Feminism and the Feminism of Ecology," in James Plant (Ed.) *Healing the Wounds: The Promise of Ecofeminism* (Santa Cruz, CA: New Society Publishers, 1989): 18–28; Ynestra King, "Healing the Wounds: Feminism, Ecology, and the Nature/Culture Divide," in Irene Diamond and Gloria F. Orenstein (Eds.), *Reweaving the World: The Emergence of Ecofeminism* (San Francisco: Sierra Club Books, 1990): 106–121; Karen J. Warren, "Feminism and Ecology: Making Connections," *Environmental Ethics*, 9 (1987): 3–21; Karen J. Warren, "Toward an Ecofeminist Ethic," *Studies in the Humanities*, 15 (1988): 140–156; Karen J. Warren, "The Power and the Promise of Ecological Feminism," *Environmental Ethics*, 12(1) (1990, Spring): 125–146; Karen J. Warren and James Cheney, "Ecological Feminism and Ecosystem Ecology," *Hypatia*, 6(1) (Spring, 1991): 179–197.
4. Vine Deloria, Jr. *Red Earth, White Lies: Native Americans and the Myth of Scientific Fact* (New York: Scribner's Sons, 1995).
5. See, for example: Naomi Klein, *This Changes Everything: Capitalism vs the Climate* (New York: Simon & Schuster, 2014).
6. Jacques Rancière discusses equality and the ways people have been advantaged due to the randomness of their birth order, for example, in *Hatred of Democracy*. S. Corcoran (Trans.) (London and New York: Verso, 2006).
7. *Babies*, also known as *Baby(ies)* and *Bébé(s)* is a French documentary film by Thomas Balmès, released in the USA by Focus Features, May 7, 2010.

8. Frederick Eby (Ed.), *Early Protestant Educators: The Educational Writings of Martin Luther, John Calvin, and Other Leaders of Protestant Thought* (New York: McGraw-Hill, 1931; New York: AMS Press, 1971).
9. J. Abner Peddiwell, *The Saber-Tooth Curriculum* (New York: McGraw-Hill, 1939, 1972, classic edition 2004).
10. Maria Montessori, *The Montessori Method* (New York: Random House, 1912, originally published in Italian in 1909). I have written extensively about Montessori and what Montessori schools are like in *Democracies Always in the Making* (Lanham: Rowman & Littlefield, 2013).
11. See Barbara J. Thayer-Bacon, *Beyond Liberal Democracy in Schools: The Power of Pluralism* (New York: Teachers College Press, 2008), Chapter 3. I use a pseudonym to refer to the school, as Diné Primary. Names are changed as well.
12. *Ibid.*, I have written about this experience in more detail on pp. 89–90.
13. *Between Sacred Mountains: Navajo Stories and Lessons from the Land* (Tucson: Sun Tracks and the University of Arizona Press, 1982, 1994).
14. Akalewold Eshete Kebede, "The Nature of Curriculum Practice in Primary Education: An Invitation to Curriculum Theorizing in the Ethiopian Context," unpublished dissertation (Addis Ababa University, defended January, 2016).

ABOUT THE AUTHOR

Barbara J. Thayer-Bacon is currently a professor of philosophy of education on the faculty of the University of Tennessee in Knoxville. She was a faculty member at Bowling Green State University from 1991–2000. She teaches courses on philosophy and history of education, cultural studies and cultural diversity, feminist theory and pedagogy. She received her Ph.D. in education from Indiana University, in 1991. Prior to that she was an elementary Montessori teacher for seven years, as well as a public school teacher for one year, and she still serves as a consultant for local schools, visiting them regularly. She is an active member in numerous professional organizations, such as the American Educational Research Association, American Educational Studies Association, Philosophy of Education Society, and International Network of Philosophers of Education and presents papers regularly at their conferences. She is past president for the Ohio Valley Philosophy of Education Society, and the Research on Women and Education and Philosophical Studies Special Interest Groups of the American Education Research Association. She has won numerous awards and served as a visiting scholar and keynote speaker multiple times. She is the first woman to serve as Editor-in-Chief of the international journal *Studies in Philosophy and Education*. She is the author of over 25 chapters in essay collections and over 50 journal articles, published in professional journals such as *The Journal of Thought*, *Educational Theory*, *Studies in Philosophy and Education*, *Inquiry*, *Educational Foundations*, and *Educational Studies*. She has written five previous books, *Philosophy Applied to Education: Nurturing a Democratic Community in the Classroom*, with Dr. Charles S. Bacon as contributing author (Upper Saddle River, NJ and Columbus, OH: Merrill Publishing, Prentice-Hall, Inc., 1998), *Transforming Critical Thinking: Constructive Thinking* (New York, NY: Teachers College Press, 2000), *Relational "(e)pistemologies"* (New York, NY: Peter Lang Publishing, Counterpoints Series, 2003), *Beyond Liberal Democracy in Schools: The Power of Pluralism* (New York, NY: Teachers College Press, 2008), and *Democracies Always in the Making: Historical and Current Philosophical Issues in Education* (Hoboken, NJ: Rowman & Littlefield, 2013), and co-edited (with Lynda Stone and Katharine Sprecher) *Education Feminism: Classic and Contemporary Readings* (New York: State University of New York Press, 2013).

INDEX

A

I

J

K

L

M

N

O

P

Q

R

S

T

U

V

W

COUNTERPOINTS

Studies in Criticality

General Editor
Shirley R. Steinberg

Counterpoints publishes the most compelling and imaginative books being written in education today. Grounded on the theoretical advances in criticalism, feminism, and postmodernism in the last two decades of the twentieth century, Counterpoints engages the meaning of these innovations in various forms of educational expression. Committed to the proposition that theoretical literature should be accessible to a variety of audiences, the series insists that its authors avoid esoteric and jargonistic languages that transform educational scholarship into an elite discourse for the initiated. Scholarly work matters only to the degree it affects consciousness and practice at multiple sites. Counterpoints' editorial policy is based on these principles and the ability of scholars to break new ground, to open new conversations, to go where educators have never gone before.

For additional information about this series or for the submission of manuscripts, please contact:

Shirley R. Steinberg
c/o Peter Lang Publishing, Inc.
29 Broadway, 18th floor
New York, New York 10006

To order other books in this series, please contact our Customer Service Department:

(800) 770-LANG (within the U.S.)
(212) 647-7706 (outside the U.S.)
(212) 647-7707 FAX

Or browse online by series:

www.peterlang.com

www.ingramcontent.com/pod-product-compliance
Ingram Content Group UK Ltd.
Pitfield, Milton Keynes, MK11 3LW, UK
UKHW021015120926
8556IPUK00040B/1158

9 781433 132223